DAILY SUMMER ACTIVITIES

BETWEEN GRADES 6 AND 7

Algonquin Area Public Library
2600 Harnish Dr.
Algonquin, IL 60102
www.aapld.org

Content Editing: Jo Ellen Moore
Andrea Weiss
Wendy Zamora
Copy Editing: Carrie Gwynne
Art Direction: Cheryl Puckett
Cover Design: Liliana Potigian
Illustrators: Greg Harris
Jim Palmer
Judith Soderquist-Cummins
Design/Production: Carolina Caird
Susan Lovell
John D. Williams

EMC 1067

Evan-Moor®
EDUCATIONAL PUBLISHERS
Helping Children Learn since 1979

**Congratulations on your
purchase of some of the
finest teaching materials
in the world.**

For information about other Evan-Moor products, call 1-800-777-4362,
fax 1-800-777-4332, or visit our Web site, www.evan-moor.com.
Entire contents © 2012 EVAN-MOOR CORP.
18 Lower Ragsdale Drive, Monterey, CA 93940-5746. Printed in USA.

Contents

Skills	Week 1	2	3	4	5	6	7	8	9	10
Reading Comprehension										
Nonfiction	●	●	●	●	●	●	●	●	●	●
Fiction	●	●	●	●	●	●	●	●	●	●
Main Idea and Details	●	●	●	●	●		●	●	●	●
Inference	●		●	●		●	●	●	●	●
Compare/Contrast		●	●	●		●		●	●	
Make Connections	●	●	●	●	●	●	●	●		●
Visualization			●			●			●	●
Sequencing		●			●				●	
Cause and Effect		●		●					●	
Prediction	●				●	●				●
Theme	●		●	●			●			●
Character and Setting		●	●	●	●	●	●	●		
Grammar/Usage/Mechanics										
Spelling	●	●	●		●	●	●	●	●	●
Abbreviation		●				●			●	
Capitalization	●	●	●	●	●	●	●	●	●	●
Punctuation	●	●	●	●	●	●	●	●	●	●
Possessives			●	●		●		●		
Quotation Marks	●	●		●	●		●	●	●	●
Singular/Plural						●			●	
Subject/Verb Agreement				●	●	●			●	●
Compound Sentences			●		●					
Syllabification								●		●
Negatives/Double Negatives	●			●						
Sentence/Fragment	●									
Independent/Dependent Clauses							●	●		
Parts of Speech:										
nouns/proper nouns	●		●	●	●		●		●	
verb phrases			●							
present, past, future verbs	●			●		●			●	●
linking verbs				●						
adjectives				●	●					●
pronouns			●				●		●	
adverbs						●				
prepositional phrases							●			
Vocabulary Development										
Clipped Words				●						
Idioms										●
Greek and Latin Roots				●						

Skills	Week 1	2	3	4	5	6	7	8	9	10
Vocabulary Development (continued)										
Base Words/Word Roots									●	
Prefixes					●		●	●		
Suffixes		●	●					●		
Homophones	●								●	
Compound Words	●									
Synonyms			●		●					
Antonyms						●				
Heteronyms			●							
Math										
Addition	●	●			●				●	
Subtraction	●	●			●				●	
Multiplication	●	●				●		●	●	●
Division	●	●	●			●		●	●	
Word Problems	●		●	●	●					
GCF/LCM		●		●						●
Exponents						●				
Fractions		●	●			●				●
Function Tables									●	
Using Graphs/Tables/Charts	●		●			●		●		
Ordered Pairs on a Graph							●		●	
Measurement:										
area			●					●		
diameter/circumference								●		
volume							●			
perimeter	●									
Decimals/Percents				●	●	●				
Polygons	●									
Range/Mean/Median/Mode						●				
Pre-Algebra									●	
Prime Factorization										●
Geography										
Physical Maps		●		●			●		●	
Political Maps			●	●		●		●		●
Latitude and Longitude	●									
Legends		●				●	●			
Projection Maps	●									
Compass Rose/Directions	●	●	●	●		●	●	●	●	●
Thinking Skills										
Riddles/Problem Solving	●	●	●	●	●	●	●	●	●	●

About This Book

What's in It

Ten Weekly Sections

Each of the 10 weekly sections contains half- and full-page activities in several subject areas, including math, geography, reading comprehension, spelling, grammar, vocabulary, and critical thinking. The practice sessions are short, giving your child a review of what was learned during the previous school year.

Each week, your child will complete the following:

Read It!	2 comprehension activities consisting of a fiction or nonfiction reading passage and 4 multiple-choice questions
Spell It	1 spelling activity practicing the week's 12 spelling words
Language Lines	2 language arts activities practicing a variety of grammar and usage skills
Write It Right	1 editing activity to correct errors in spelling, grammar, and punctuation
Vocabulary	1 activity for building vocabulary and practicing such skills as compound words, word parts, synonyms, and homographs
Math Time	3 math activities on skills including word problems, fractions, and measurements
Geography	1 map activity testing basic geography concepts
In My Own Words	2 creative-writing exercises
Mind Jigglers	1 critical-thinking activity
Weekly Record Form	a place to record the most memorable moment of the week, as well as a reading log for recording the number of minutes spent reading each day

How to Use It

The short practice sessions in *Daily Summer Activities* act as a bridge between grades, preparing your child for the coming school year by keeping him or her fresh on the concepts and skills mastered this past year. After completing the book, your child will feel more confident as he or she progresses to the next grade. You can help by following the suggestions below to ensure your child's success.

Provide Time and Space

Make sure that your child has a quiet place for completing the activities. The practice session should be short and successful. Consider your child's personality and other activities as you decide how and where to schedule daily practice periods.

Provide Encouragement and Support

Your response is important to your child's feelings of success. Keep your remarks positive and recognize the effort your child has made. Correct mistakes together. Work toward independence, guiding practice when necessary.

Check In Each Week

Use the weekly record sheet to talk about the most memorable moments and learning experiences of the week and to discuss the literature your child is reading.

Be a Model Reader

The most important thing you can do is to make sure your child sees *you* reading. Read books, magazines, and newspapers. Visit libraries and bookstores. Point out interesting signs, maps, and advertisements wherever you go. Even though your child is an independent reader, you can still share the reading experience by discussing what you read every day.

Go on Learning Excursions

Learning takes place everywhere and through many kinds of experiences. Build learning power over the summer by:

➤ visiting local museums and historic sites. Use a guidebook or search online to find points of interest in your area. The Chamber of Commerce and AAA are good sources of information about local attractions.

➤ collecting art materials and working together to create a collage, mobile, or scrapbook.

➤ going to a play, concert, or other show at a local theater or performance center.

➤ creating a movie of your child's favorite story. Write a simple script, make basic costumes and props, and recruit friends and family members to be the actors. Practice until everyone is comfortable before shooting the video.

➤ planting a garden. If you are short on space, plant in containers.

Spell It

A
absent-minded
acceptable
admitted
advised
amazement
amphibian
answered
Antarctica
anywhere
applied
archeology
assistance
assistants

B
beliefs
bilingual
binoculars
bipedal
boundaries
brainstorm

C
careful
cartographer
castle
centennial
centipede
chalkboard
cheerful
chieftain
circumference
committee
complement
compliment
concluded
condemn
coughing
credit card

D
demanded
doorknob
doubtful

E
echoes
efficient
effortless
embarrass
enjoyment
environment
everybody
exaggerate
exceed
exhaustion

F
fantasy
finally
finely
flexible
foreword
forward

G
government
grateful

H
halves
headquarters
hemisphere
honorable
humorless

I
ice cream
inquired
insisted
international
interrupt

J
journeys
judgment

M
meanwhile
mosquitoes

O
occasion
occurrence
old-fashioned
opportunity
outstanding

P
pamphlet
parallel
parallelogram
passersby
patience
patients
patriotism
peninsula
perpendicular
phenomenal
plumber
pneumonia
powerless
preferred
profession

R
recommend
replied
rhombus

S
schedules
semiannual
semicircle
shipwreck
signpost
stomachache
stationary
stationery
substances
sweatshirt
symphony

T
thieves
thoughtful
tireless
tomatoes
toughest
triad
triathlon
triceps
twelfth
typhoid

U
unify
unique

V
varieties

W
whined
whispered
wholesome

WEEK 1

Check off each box as you complete the day's work.

⌐ **ALL WEEK**

⌐ **MONDAY**

⌐ **TUESDAY**

⌐ **WEDNESDAY**

⌐ **THURSDAY**

⌐ **FRIDAY**

Spelling Words

absent-minded

anywhere

brainstorm

credit card

everybody

headquarters

ice cream

meanwhile

old-fashioned

outstanding

stomachache

sweatshirt

Get Creative!

Turn this scribble into an octopus.

A Memorable Moment

What sticks in your mind about this week? Write about it.

_____

_____

_____

_____

_____

_____

_____

Reading Record

	Book Title	Pages	Time
Monday			
Tuesday			
Wednesday			
Thursday			
Friday			

Describe a character you read about this week.

_____

_____

_____

_____

_____

_____

Read the article. Then answer the questions.

An American Treasure

Floating, airborne, and *focused*—these words have often been used to describe how Julius "Dr. J" Erving played basketball. Erving became one of the best players in the sport. He forever changed the way people played basketball.

Erving started playing professional basketball in the 1970s. The sport was different then. It was mainly a floor game, with players running back and forth across the court. Unlike other players, Erving found that his skill was in the air, because he could leap far and high. He soon became known for his slam-dunks, which were not as common in the 1970s as they are today. Most players scored by throwing the ball toward the basket from far away. But Erving flew toward the backboard with the ball in hand, spinning his body in the air before sending the ball down through the hoop. This tremendous skill helped the teams he played for win three championships.

Dr. J says of his life, "I saw that basketball could be my way out, and I worked hard to make sure it was." This inspiring athlete discovered his unique skill early on and used it to his advantage throughout his life.

. . . .

1. **How does the author probably feel about Julius Erving?**

   Ⓐ disappointed

   Ⓑ inspired

   Ⓒ puzzled

   Ⓓ worried

2. **In what way was Dr. J different from other basketball players?**

   Ⓐ in the number of points he scored

   Ⓑ in the way he moved through the air

   Ⓒ in the number of championships he won

   Ⓓ in how old he was when he played

3. **What is probably the reason that the author wrote "An American Treasure"?**

   Ⓐ to explain how basketball has changed

   Ⓑ to describe the history of basketball

   Ⓒ to entertain readers with a basketball story

   Ⓓ to tell about a great basketball player

4. **Which statement is *not* a theme of the passage?**

   Ⓐ Basketball is an amazing sport.

   Ⓑ Dr. J worked hard at basketball.

   Ⓒ Erving changed basketball as a sport.

   Ⓓ Dr. J was best known for his slam-dunks.

Write It Right

Rewrite each sentence and correct the errors.

1. Wernt their no milk in the refrijerator

_____

2. there going to come to sea me at six oclock

_____

3. antonio was to big for his bike sew he sold it at red barn flee market

_____

4. oh no katied cried i left my cell phone at skool

_____

MATH TIME

Solve the math problems.

8,376	5,268	1,425	8,605
+ 6,825	+ 9,706	+ 5,285	+ 3,497

4,625	5,215	6,850	9,605
− 1,709	− 2,166	− 2,279	− 4,238

839	456	1,823	7,069
x 72	x 18	x 56	x 56

49)2,450   33)7,095   71)3,692   62)26,040

SPELL IT

A **compound word** can be open, closed, or hyphenated.
sea level   **makeup**   **friendly-looking**

Use one word from each box to make the spelling words for the week.

every	ache
old	minded
brain	standing
sweat	quarters
ice	card
credit	cream
head	while
out	where
mean	shirt
stomach	body
any	storm
absent	fashioned

1. _____   7. _____

2. _____   8. _____

3. _____   9. _____

4. _____   10. _____

5. _____   11. _____

6. _____   12. _____

In My Own Words

If you were granted a superpower, which one would you choose?
Explain your choice.

LANGUAGE LINES

Nouns name people, places, things, or ideas. A **singular** noun names one person, place, thing, or idea. A **plural** noun names more than one.

Cross out the noun in each sentence that is in the wrong form and write the correct form above it. Then circle all the other nouns in the sentence.

1. Both the boys and the girls in our class have many pet.

2. One individuals brought a surprise to school for her friends.

3. It was a photos of kittens that her family could not keep.

4. There was a yellow basket with two white kitten inside.

5. Several students asked if the class could adopt an animals.

6. The teacher suggested learning about whales and other endangered creature.

MATH TIME

Solve the word problems about the pet store.

1. The pet store has 8 rabbits for sale. Each morning, the owner feeds the rabbits a total of 2 cups of pellets. If each rabbit receives the same amount of pellets, how much does each rabbit receive?

2. On Monday, there were 92 fish in the fish tank. On Tuesday, 4 fish were sold. On Wednesday, 1 fish was sold. On Thursday, 4 fish were added to the tank, and on Friday, 3 fish were sold. How many fish were in the fish tank at the end of the week?

Answer: _____

Answer: _____

Read the story. Then answer the questions.

A Long Day

Jamie was tired. She had been on her feet for hours. Her mom owned a small but busy restaurant in town. Three of her mom's employees had called in sick that morning. There was a big festival in the city park that day, and Jamie had wanted to go. But her mom had asked for her help at the restaurant.

All Jamie wanted to do was sit down for a while. Instead, she hurried around the restaurant, taking orders and refilling coffee cups. As soon as one table was cleared, a new set of customers walked in. The customers just kept coming! That meant more orders and more coffee.

"Order up!" called the cook from the kitchen. Jamie stared at the kitchen door. She thought about all of the food stalls at the festival. Cooks there were preparing special foods from all over the world. Jamie imagined the delicious smells of new and exotic foods.

"Hurry, Jamie!" the cook called, catching Jamie lost in thought.

"I'm coming," Jamie grumbled. But her mom had already picked up the plates of hot food from the counter and delivered them to a table by the window.

"Wake up, Jamie," her mom said. "I know you don't want to be here, but I need your help."

· ·

1. **Why is Jamie daydreaming?**

   Ⓐ She is half asleep.

   Ⓑ She has nothing better to do.

   Ⓒ She would rather be working in the kitchen.

   Ⓓ She wants to be somewhere else.

2. **What will most likely happen next in the story?**

   Ⓐ The cook will quit.

   Ⓑ Jamie will leave and go to the festival.

   Ⓒ Jamie will become busy again.

   Ⓓ Jamie's mom will close the restaurant.

3. **What will Jamie most likely do when she gets home?**

   Ⓐ make dinner for her mom

   Ⓑ go for a walk

   Ⓒ see if the festival is still going on

   Ⓓ apply for a waitress job

4. **What is the main idea of the story?**

   Ⓐ Festivals are more fun than work.

   Ⓑ It is important to daydream.

   Ⓒ Owning a restaurant is difficult.

   Ⓓ We cannot always do what we want to do.

Vo·cab·u·lar·y

Homophones are words that sound alike but have different spellings and different meanings. Be sure to use the correct spelling for the meaning you intend.

They're over **there** eating **their** lunch.

You're not taking **your** shoes off, are you?

A. Circle the correct homophone for each clue.

1.	belonging to someone	who's	whose
2.	a location	site	sight
3.	short for "you are"	your	you're
4.	to cut off	sheer	shear
5.	at that place	there	their
6.	to agree	ascent	assent
7.	short for "who is"	who's	whose
8.	belonging to them	they're	their
9.	the ability to see	site	sight
10.	extreme or steep	sheer	shear
11.	an upward movement	ascent	assent
12.	belonging to it	its	it's

B. Write two sentences, each using a pair of homophones from Activity A. Do not repeat the examples above.

1. _____

    _____

2. _____

    _____

LANGUAGE LINES

A **sentence** must express a complete thought. A group of words that does not express a complete thought is called a **fragment**.

Read each group of words and decide whether it expresses a complete thought. Circle *sentence* if the group of words expresses a complete thought. Circle *fragment* if it does not.

1. Glaciers cover approximately 10 percent of Earth's land.   sentence   fragment

2. Icebergs break away from glaciers.   sentence   fragment

3. The largest masses of ice on Earth.   sentence   fragment

4. A moving glacier drags earth and gravel with it.   sentence   fragment

5. Very destructive.   sentence   fragment

6. Formed valleys and lakes in many places on Earth.   sentence   fragment

7. Scientists study glaciers.   sentence   fragment

8. Record of changes in the climate.   sentence   fragment

In My Own Words

You want your own laptop computer. Your parents don't think you need one at your age. What would you say to change their minds?

Mind Jigglers

Ancient Egypt

A. People in ancient Egypt used symbols called "hieroglyphics" for their written language. Use the hieroglyphic alphabet to complete the writing activities below.

HIEROGLYPHIC ALPHABET

A eagle	B leg	C (hard c) basket / (soft c) folded cloth	D hand	E two reed flowers	F horned viper	G a stand for a jar
H reed shelter	**I** reed flower	**J** snake	**K** basket	**L** lion	**M** owl	**N** water
O lasso	**P** stool	**Q** hill	**R** mouth	**S** folded cloth	**T** a loaf of bread	**U** chick
V horned viper	**W** chick	**X** sounds like *k + s* as in *six*	**Y** two reed flowers	**Z** a bolt	**CH** tethering rope	**SH** pond

B. Write your name in hieroglyphics.

C. Now try writing a sentence or two. When you are finished, show your paper to a friend and ask him or her to translate your hieroglyphics.

MATH TIME

Neighborhood Yard Sale

Read the bar graph showing the amount of money ten families earned at a yard sale. Then use the graph to answer the questions.

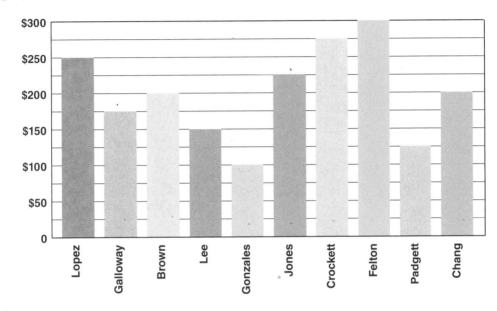

1. Which family earned the most money at the yard sale? _____

2. What is the difference in dollar amount between the most money earned and the least money earned? _____

3. What was the total amount earned by the families at the neighborhood yard sale? _____

4. What was the average amount earned by a family at the yard sale? _____

> **Remember:**
> To calculate an **average**, add all the items together and then divide by the number of items.
>
> **The sum of 3, 5, 7, and 1 is 16.**
>
> **16 ÷ 4 = 4**
>
> **The average is 4.**

Projection Map

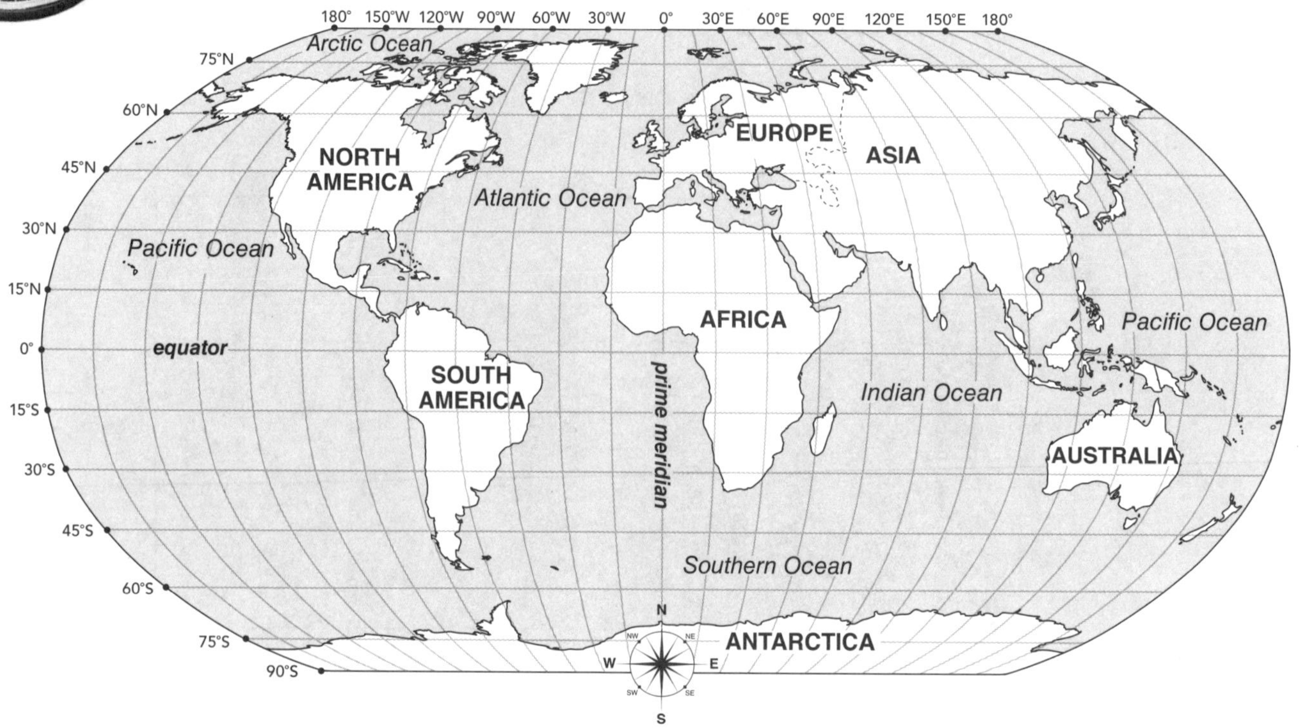

Use the map to answer the questions.

1. The longitude 150°W passes through how many continents? _____

2. Which line of latitude is located at 0°? _____

3. Europe is immediately west of which continent? _____

4. Which three continents does the prime meridian run through?

_____

5. Which three continents does the latitude 20°S run through?

_____

WEEK 2

Check off each box as you complete the day's work.

Spelling Words

admitted

advised

answered

applied

concluded

demanded

inquired

insisted

preferred

replied

whined

whispered

Get Creative!

Draw a picture for the caption.

"Hark! Who goes there?"

A Memorable Moment

What sticks in your mind about this week? Write about it.

_____

_____

_____

_____

_____

_____

_____

Reading Record

	Book Title	Pages	Time
Monday			
Tuesday			
Wednesday			
Thursday			
Friday			

Describe a character you read about this week.

_____

_____

_____

_____

_____

_____

© Evan-Moor Corp. • EMC 1067 • Daily Summer Activities

Read the article. Then answer the questions.

Dirty Job? Oh Yeah!

"You couldn't pay me to do that job!" Have you ever said that? Some occupations are so gross that most people would never be willing to do them.

Jeff Biggs has a job like that, but he likes it. He's the kind of guy who, as a kid, loved to slosh around in mud after a rainstorm, the kind of kid who loved squeezing oatmeal through his fingers.

Biggs's dirty job is being a sewer inspector. "Believe me," says Biggs, "gross doesn't come close to describing it. I creep, sometimes swim, through sewage all day." Biggs inspects city sewers that carry household wastewater and storm-drain runoff to water treatment plants. In addition to the unpleasant smells that he encounters, sewer tunnels are home to creatures such as cockroaches and rats. And these creatures aren't shy.

What is it like to do a really disgusting job day after day? "Someone has to do it," says Biggs. "I seriously can't imagine sitting in an office all day, and I earn a good salary. At the end of my workday, I've accomplished something, and I've helped to keep our city's water clean and drinkable."

And after work? "I don't walk into the house right away," explains Biggs. "We installed the washing machine in the garage and put a shower stall in there, too. I toss my clothes into the washer, take a shower, and dress in clean clothes. Then I greet my family. Of course, sometimes the clothes go into the trash, not the washer."

1. **Which adjectives best describe Jeff Biggs?**

   Ⓐ flashy, conceited, loud

   Ⓑ positive, upbeat, thoughtful

   Ⓒ smart, wealthy, nervous

   Ⓓ negative, shy, withdrawn

2. **Which adjective best describes the setting in which Biggs works?**

   Ⓐ disgusting

   Ⓑ boring

   Ⓒ pleasant

   Ⓓ appealing

3. **Which sentence best describes the central message of the passage?**

   Ⓐ Biggs's job embarrasses him.

   Ⓑ Biggs cannot imagine having a nicer job.

   Ⓒ Biggs is proud of the work he does.

   Ⓓ Biggs is just doing his job until he gets a better one.

4. **Which job would Jeff Biggs probably most enjoy?**

   Ⓐ being a lawyer

   Ⓑ being a poet

   Ⓒ being a computer programmer

   Ⓓ being a plumber

Write It Right

Rewrite each sentence and correct the errors.

1. my freind mr murphy visited churchs in canada china and japan

_____

2. there mom ask them to go to browns market for her

_____

3. why due i have to due my home work now asked tori

_____

4. gary the custodien unlocked the supply closit for the teachers mrs day

_____

MATH TIME

Solve the mixed-number addition and subtraction problems.

1. $2\frac{1}{3} + 4\frac{2}{3} =$ _____

2. $5\frac{3}{8} + \frac{2}{8} =$ _____

3. $4\frac{3}{7} + 2\frac{5}{7} =$ _____

4. $4\frac{2}{5} + 3\frac{1}{10} =$ _____

5. $3\frac{5}{8} + 6\frac{3}{4} =$ _____

6. $2\frac{2}{3} + 4\frac{1}{2} =$ _____

7. $2\frac{2}{3} - 1\frac{2}{3} =$ _____

8. $6\frac{4}{5} - 1\frac{1}{5} =$ _____

9. $4\frac{2}{3} - 1\frac{1}{2} =$ _____

10. $8\frac{3}{4} - 3\frac{1}{3} =$ _____

11. $9\frac{1}{3} - 4\frac{1}{2} =$ _____

12. $7\frac{2}{5} - 2\frac{1}{3} =$ _____

SPELL IT

> The past tense of most verbs is formed by adding **–ed**. Sometimes you must make a spelling change before adding the **–ed** ending.

Add –ed to each word to write the spelling words for the week. Check the box under the rule you used.

	no change	double the last consonant	change y to i	drop the silent e
1. admit _____				
2. demand _____				
3. reply _____				
4. whine _____				
5. insist _____				
6. advise _____				
7. prefer _____				
8. whisper _____				
9. conclude _____				
10. answer _____				
11. apply _____				
12. inquire _____				

In My Own Words

Write a rhyming poem about your favorite color.

LANGUAGE LINES

An **abbreviation** is a short way of writing a word or a group of words.

A. Write the abbreviation for each group of words. (Hint: The abbreviations for these words are *not* usually written with periods.) The first one has been done for you.

1. North Atlantic Treaty Organization: ___NATO___

2. United Nations: _____

3. Central Intelligence Agency: _____

4. as soon as possible: _____

5. miles per hour: _____

6. New York: _____

B. Write the word that each underlined abbreviation stands for.

1. Washington <u>Ave.</u>: _____

2. 179 West Road, <u>Apt.</u> 24: _____

3. 1 <u>oz.</u> milk: _____

4. <u>p.</u> 199: _____

MATH TIME

Complete the multiplication problems.

> **Remember:**
>
> To multiply mixed numbers, change the mixed number to an improper fraction.
>
> $$2\frac{1}{2} \times 2\frac{2}{3} = \frac{5}{2} \times \frac{8}{3}$$
>
> Then multiply the fractions and simplify the answer.
>
> $$\frac{5 \times 8}{2 \times 3} = \frac{40}{6} = 6\frac{4}{6} = 6\frac{2}{3}$$

1. $\frac{2}{5} \times \frac{1}{3} =$ _____

2. $\frac{1}{4} \times \frac{3}{7} =$ _____

3. $\frac{1}{2} \times \frac{3}{8} =$ _____

4. $\frac{4}{9} \times \frac{1}{2} =$ _____

5. $1\frac{2}{5} \times 3\frac{3}{4} =$ _____

6. $4\frac{2}{7} \times \frac{1}{2} =$ _____

7. $3\frac{3}{5} \times 2\frac{6}{7} =$ _____

8. $5\frac{1}{3} \times 4\frac{3}{7} =$ _____

Read the story. Then answer the questions.

The Rafting Trip

Tina took the helmet from Dale, the rafting instructor who would be guiding the group down the river. Tina pushed her hair out of her face and fitted the helmet on her head. Then she fastened the strap. "I've never had to wear a helmet on a boat before," she complained.

"This isn't really a boat," said Dale. "It's a raft," he explained in a casual tone. "A raft is filled with air and it doesn't have an engine." Dale picked up a stack of life jackets and began distributing them to people as they waited to climb into the raft. "We'll hit some choppy water in the river," he told everyone. "And we want all of you to be safe."

"But I feel silly in this helmet," Tina said. "Do I really need it?" Stepping forward to get a life jacket, she caught her foot in a rope that was coiled up near the raft. Tina stumbled forward in surprise and, with a shriek, fell down onto the pile of rope.

Dale smiled at Tina as she untangled herself. "Yes, you really do need it," he answered, holding out his hand to help Tina up.

Tina stood up carefully. "You know," she said, "I think you're right."

. . . .

1. **What caused Tina to fall?**

   Ⓐ getting tangled in the raft's rope

   Ⓑ not being able to see out of her helmet

   Ⓒ tripping on a life jacket

   Ⓓ hitting some choppy water

2. **What did Dale do immediately after giving everyone their helmets?**

   Ⓐ He asked if anyone wanted a life jacket.

   Ⓑ He helped Tina stand up again.

   Ⓒ He picked up life jackets to hand out.

   Ⓓ He took a helmet from Tina.

3. **Why did Dale want everyone to wear a helmet?**

   Ⓐ because he knew Tina would trip

   Ⓑ because he thought rafts were more dangerous than boats

   Ⓒ because he did not have enough life jackets

   Ⓓ because he wanted everyone to be safe

4. **What was the effect of Tina's fall?**

   Ⓐ Dale let Tina remove her helmet.

   Ⓑ Dale decided to be more careful with rope.

   Ⓒ Tina decided the helmet was silly.

   Ⓓ Tina realized she needed the helmet.

Vo·cab·u·lar·y

A **phobia** is a very strong fear of something. The words in the box are examples of phobias.

aquaphobia	astrophobia	cyclophobia	bibliophobia
cyberphobia	chronophobia	papyrophobia	ambulophobia
botanophobia	arithmophobia	arachnophobia	triskaidekaphobia

Use the names of the phobias in the box above to answer each question below.

1. If the root **aqua** means "water," what is the fear of water? _____

2. If the root **chron** means "time," what is the fear of time? _____

3. If **botany** is the study of plants, what is the fear of plants? _____

4. If the root **biblio** means "book," what is the fear of books? _____

5. If the root **astro** means "star," what is the fear of stars? _____

6. If **ambulate** is a synonym for **walk**, what is the fear of walking? _____

7. If spiders belong to the **arachnid** class, what is the fear of spiders? _____

8. If **arithmetic** is a synonym for **math**, what is the fear of numbers? _____

9. If the root **cycl** means "circle" or "wheels," what is the fear of bicycles? _____

10. If **cyber** means "relating to computers," what is the fear of computers? _____

11. If **papyrus** was used by ancient civilizations to write on, what is the fear of paper? _____

12. If **triskaideka** is the Greek word for "thirteen," what is the fear of the number 13? _____

LANGUAGE LINES

The topic sentence introduces the main idea of a paragraph.

Read the paragraph and underline the topic sentence. Then summarize the main idea and list three supporting details below it.

Seeds spread themselves around in many different ways. Some seeds move on the wind. They have winglike parts to catch the wind. Other seeds have hooks or stickers. They latch onto the fur of animals and are carried away as the animals roam. Some seeds disperse themselves by floating on water. We humans move seeds, too, when we plant them in our yards and gardens.

Main Idea:

_____

Details:

1. _____

2. _____

3. _____

In My Own Words

What do you think is the most important human invention ever created? Explain your choice.

Mind Jigglers

In My Room

A. Write four adjectives to describe your room.

1. _____   3. _____

2. _____   4. _____

What is...

the oldest thing in your room? _____

the newest thing in your room? _____

the thing in your room you most treasure? _____

something in your room you have outgrown? _____

B. Use the clues to name things you would probably find in a bedroom. Then find the words in the word search. Words may appear across, down, or diagonally.

where you dream   _____

where clothes hang   _____

taped to a wall   _____

a homework surface   _____

a head cushion   _____

gives you a view   _____

a place for books   _____

has a bulb   _____

has a seat   _____

R	B	A	D	R	C	B
M	L	E	I	B	L	P
T	P	A	D	A	O	S
X	H	O	G	S	S	H
C	D	E	S	M	E	E
P	H	E	A	T	T	L
I	R	P	S	O	E	F
L	O	Z	P	K	E	R
L	W	I	N	D	O	W
O	L	E	H	C	A	R
W	L	A	M	P	I	J

MATH TIME

Reducing Fractions

One way to reduce fractions to their lowest terms is to divide the numerator and the denominator by their Greatest Common Factor (GCF). The GCF is the highest number that divides exactly into two or more numbers.

> The GCF of **4** and **20** is **4**. Divide both the numerator and denominator by **4**.
>
> $$\frac{4}{20} = \frac{4 \div 4}{20 \div 4} = \frac{1}{5}$$

Find the GCF of each numerator and denominator. Then reduce the fraction, if possible.

1. $\frac{3}{9}$ GCF=_____ _____

2. $\frac{4}{12}$ GCF=_____ _____

3. $\frac{5}{10}$ GCF=_____ _____

4. $\frac{15}{20}$ GCF=_____ _____

5. $\frac{4}{7}$ GCF=_____ _____

6. $\frac{25}{70}$ GCF=_____ _____

7. $\frac{2}{6}$ GCF=_____ _____

8. $\frac{12}{15}$ GCF=_____ _____

9. $\frac{20}{24}$ GCF=_____ _____

10. $\frac{15}{45}$ GCF=_____ _____

11. $\frac{36}{42}$ GCF=_____ _____

12. $\frac{42}{56}$ GCF=_____ _____

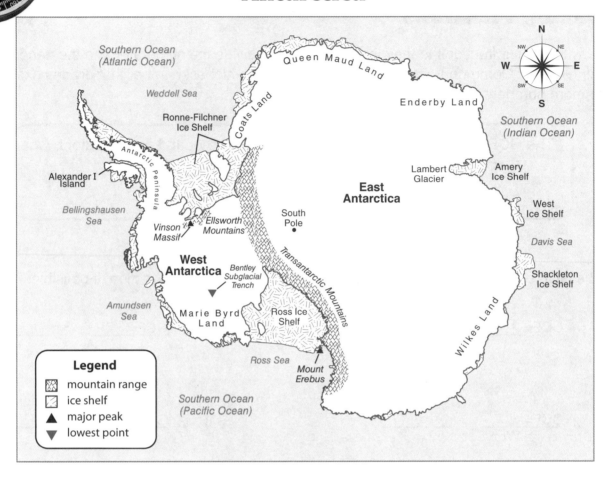

Geography

Antarctica

1. Which mountain range runs through the middle of the continent? _____

2. What is the name of the major peak just south of the Ronne-Filchner Ice Shelf? _____

3. What is the name of the mountain peak bordering the Ross Ice Shelf? _____

4. Which ice shelf is closest to the Lambert Glacier? _____

5. What is the name of the peninsula in West Antarctica? _____

6. What is the name of the lowest point in Antarctica? _____

West of Greenwich   Longitude West of Greenwich

| A | 120° | B | 150° | C | 180° | D | 150° | E | 120° | F | 90° |

WEEK
3

Check off each box as you complete the day's work.

Spelling Words

amazement

careful

cheerful

effortless

enjoyment

government

grateful

humorless

judgment

powerless

thoughtful

tireless

Get Creative!

Draw your favorite kind of pet.

A Memorable Moment

What sticks in your mind about this week? Write about it.

_____

_____

_____

_____

_____

_____

Reading Record

	Book Title	Pages	Time
Monday	_____	____	____
Tuesday	_____	____	____
Wednesday	_____	____	____
Thursday	_____	____	____
Friday	_____	____	____

Describe a character you read about this week.

_____

_____

_____

_____

_____

Read the story. Then answer the questions.

Natural Entertainment

When the days grew long in the middle of summer, Leticia liked to go to the park, stretch out on her back, and watch the clouds. Sometimes the clouds looked like animals, everyday objects, or people she knew. One thing was certain—clouds never stayed in place for long.

One day, Leticia saw a cloud that looked like a dragon. After a few minutes, it changed from a standing dragon to a flying dragon. Then it appeared to change direction. Another cloud floated in to mix with it, and the dragon turned into a dancing penguin with a hat. Then it turned into a sitting dog, then a barking dog, then an alligator. "This is better than TV!" Leticia proclaimed.

Mr. Espinosa, the music teacher at Leticia's school, was flying a kite with his children at the other end of the park. He recognized Leticia's voice. He gave the spool of kite string to his son and went over to greet Leticia.

"Hi, Mr. Espinosa!" Leticia said. "Look at those clouds. They keep changing! First they looked like a dragon, then a penguin, then a dog, and now an alligator!"

Mr. Espinosa looked up. "An alligator?" he said. "That looks like a speedboat to me."

Leticia looked again. He was right! "How do clouds know how to make so many shapes?"

"It's a mystery," answered Mr. Espinosa. "Definitely better than TV, though."

"Definitely," Leticia said, as the speedboat turned into a chicken.

. . . .

1. **Which one did Leticia *not* see in the clouds?**

   Ⓐ a teacher

   Ⓑ a dog

   Ⓒ a chicken

   Ⓓ a dragon

2. **Which statement best expresses the main idea of the story?**

   Ⓐ Penguins can turn into alligators.

   Ⓑ Mr. Espinosa visited the park with his children.

   Ⓒ Clouds can stir the imagination.

   Ⓓ Everyone should watch television.

3. **Why did Mr. Espinosa come to the park?**

   Ⓐ to meet with his students

   Ⓑ to fly a kite with his children

   Ⓒ to look at clouds

   Ⓓ to walk his dog

4. **Which idea goes with the story and is also suggested by the title?**

   Ⓐ Kite flying is a way to have fun without technology.

   Ⓑ Watching clouds change shape is fun.

   Ⓒ Dogs and alligators get along very well.

   Ⓓ Watching TV is naturally entertaining.

Write It Right

Rewrite each sentence and correct the errors.

1. will you help them guys paint there fence

_____

_____

2. we red articles from newsweek time and the wall street journal

_____

_____

3. while she was poring tee the girl spilt some on her mothers table

_____

_____

MATH TIME

Complete each of the following division problems. Write your answer in the simplest form. The first one has been done for you.

1. $2\frac{1}{5} \div 1\frac{1}{2} =$ ___$1\frac{7}{15}$___

$$\frac{11}{5} \div \frac{3}{2} = \frac{11}{5} \times \frac{2}{3} = \frac{22}{15}$$

4. $4\frac{1}{3} \div 6\frac{2}{3} =$ _____

7. $2\frac{3}{5} \div 2\frac{1}{5} =$ _____

2. $3\frac{3}{4} \div 1\frac{1}{3} =$ _____

5. $3\frac{1}{2} \div 4\frac{1}{2} =$ _____

8. $8\frac{1}{2} \div 4\frac{1}{5} =$ _____

3. $2\frac{1}{2} \div 1\frac{1}{4} =$ _____

6. $7\frac{1}{2} \div 8 =$ _____

9. $9\frac{4}{5} \div 6\frac{2}{5} =$ _____

SPELL IT

A **suffix** is a word part added to the end
of a word that changes its meaning.

Add the suffix *–ment, –ful,* or *–less* to each base word to make the spelling word for the week.
Then circle the base word that could be joined with another suffix to make a new word.
Write the new word next to the spelling word.

1. govern _____

2. tire _____

3. thought _____

4. amaze _____

5. humor _____

6. cheer _____

7. effort _____

8. judg _____

9. grate _____

10. care _____

11. power _____

12. enjoy _____

In My Own Words

If you found a magic cell phone that allowed you to talk to anyone—alive, dead, real, or fictional—whom would you call and why? What would you say?

LANGUAGE LINES

Combine the sentences to make one sentence.

1. Marilyn bought some sandals. She tried on hiking boots, walking shoes, and ballet slippers.

   _____

   _____

2. We drove to the camping store to buy a tent cover. When we got there, the store was closed.

   _____

   _____

3. Jo went to visit her sister. Jo's sister lives in St. Louis. Jo has only one sister.

   _____

   _____

4. I found a carton of eggs in the refrigerator. It had only one egg in it. I couldn't make cookies.

   _____

   _____

MATH TIME

Solve the word problems about pizza.

1. Tim has one-half of a pizza that he wants to divide equally between two people. Draw a picture of this problem to show how much pizza each person will get. Write the math sentence that goes with the problem.

2. George has three-fourths of a pizza. He is going to divide it into six equal slices. Draw a picture of this problem to show how much of the whole pizza each slice will be. Write the math sentence that goes with the problem.

Answer: _____

Answer: _____

Read the article. Then answer the questions.

World Champion Magician

As a young girl growing up in China, Juliana Chen never imagined the success she would have as a performer. At just 10 years old, she was chosen to attend the Hunan Academy for the Performing Arts. The Hunan Academy is one of China's best schools for dancers, acrobats, and other kinds of performers.

Juliana first trained in ballet. Then she studied juggling and acrobatics and joined a famous acrobatic troupe. But the work was physically difficult, and Juliana injured her leg several times. While she was recovering from one of her injuries, Juliana watched a magic show on television. That's when Juliana knew she would become a magician.

Juliana impressed people with her special skill. Because of her acrobatic training, she was skilled with her body and her hands. She could make cards appear out of thin air, it seemed. In 1986, Juliana won the All-China Best Magician competition.

After her success in China, Juliana immigrated to Canada. There, she became an even bigger star. Soon, she traveled around the world, learning new tricks and performing in front of royalty. In 1997, she became the first woman and the first magician from China to win a world title for a solo act at the World Congress of Magicians, a major competition for magicians. Juliana continues to teach, perform, win awards, and learn new magic tricks.

. . . .

1. **Why did Juliana Chen become a magician?**

   Ⓐ She did not like ballet.

   Ⓑ She was not successful as an acrobat.

   Ⓒ She was injured as an acrobat.

   Ⓓ She wanted to move to Canada.

2. **What is one theme of the passage?**

   Ⓐ Magic is a sport.

   Ⓑ Doing something you enjoy can bring many rewards.

   Ⓒ It is better to try something new than to keep doing the same old thing.

   Ⓓ Teaching others is the most satisfying work.

3. **In what way are ballet, juggling, and acrobatics alike?**

   Ⓐ They all involve competition.

   Ⓑ They are all performing arts.

   Ⓒ They are all easy to learn.

   Ⓓ They have nothing in common.

4. **What inference can you make about Juliana Chen?**

   Ⓐ She dislikes being around others.

   Ⓑ She is shy and private.

   Ⓒ She is fun-loving and not very serious.

   Ⓓ She works hard to achieve her goals.

Vo·cab·u·lar·y

Synonyms are words that have the same or nearly the same meaning.

  Funny and **humorous** are *synonyms.*

Heteronyms are words that are spelled the same but have different meanings and pronunciations.

  Desert (a dry region) and **desert** (to withdraw from or abandon) are *heteronyms.*

A. Simon has something interesting to tell you. To find out what it is, do what Simon says—and *only* what Simon says.

1. Simon says, "Cross off all synonyms for **eat** in column C and in row three."

2. Simon says, "Cross off all country names."

3. Simon says, "Cross off all words in column D and in row 5 that could be heteronyms."

4. Cross off all words that contain a vowel.

5. Simon says, "Cross off all words in column A that refer to people."

6. Simon says, "Cross off all compound words in row six and in column E."

7. Simon says, "Cross off all words with fewer than three letters."

	A	B	C	D	E	F
1	Canada	If	consume	American	overcook	we
2	artists	colonists	it	object	Germany	ate
3	popcorn	nibble	feast	conduct	like	gobble
4	doctors	Japan	cereal	separate	watermelon	with
5	students	as	dine	milk	desert	and
6	milkshake	sugar	munch	cupcake	mealtime	Mexico

B. Write out the remaining ten words to discover a fascinating fact.

_____

_____

LANGUAGE LINES

The **complete subject** of a sentence includes the main noun or pronoun and related words. The **complete predicate** contains the verb and related words.

Underline the complete subject, and circle the complete predicate. The first one has been done for you.

1. <u>My world studies class</u> (is planning an international dinner.)

2. Our teacher will make an exotic dish.

3. Mr. Crosby has offered to bring chicken curry with rice.

4. Curry is a mixture of spices popular in India.

5. My friend Rachel is bringing a Hungarian dish with noodles.

6. My mother might help me make fried okra.

7. Fried okra is a popular vegetable dish in the southern United States.

8. All of the seventh and eighth graders are invited to the dinner.

9. Our principal, Ms. Rodriguez, can't be there.

10. Ms. Rodriguez and her husband are going on a trip to Spain.

In My Own Words

What would you do if you found a wallet that contained $100, and there was no name and address in it?

Mind Jigglers

Friends

Use the names in the box to match each character below with his or her friend.

Abu	Jill	Ron	Sam	Toto	Jane	Dale
Ernie	Luigi	Clark	Juliet	Piglet	Robin	Barbie
Timon	Louise	Wendy	Scooby	Wilbur	Minnie	Tweety
Barney	Watson	Patrick	Donkey	Milhouse	Woodstock	Daffy Duck

1. Batman & _____

2. Chip & _____

3. Thelma & _____

4. Sherlock & _____

5. Harry & _____

6. Charlotte & _____

7. Bugs Bunny & _____

8. SpongeBob & _____

9. Bert & _____

10. Jack & _____

11. Shrek & _____

12. Lewis & _____

13. Mario & _____

14. Frodo & _____

15. Pooh & _____

16. Shaggy & _____

17. Romeo & _____

18. Pumbaa & _____

19. Tarzan & _____

20. Peter Pan & _____

21. Fred & _____

22. Mickey & _____

23. Dorothy & _____

24. Snoopy & _____

25. Bart & _____

26. Aladdin & _____

27. Ken & _____

28. Sylvester & _____

MATH TIME

Find the **area**.

1. _____

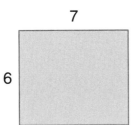

7

6

2. _____

4

4

3. _____

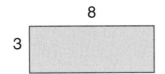

8

3

4. _____

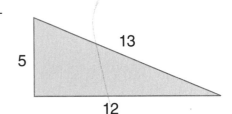

5

8

5. _____

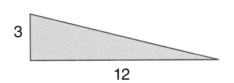

3

12

Find the **perimeter**.

1. _____

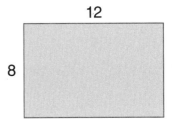

12

8

2. _____

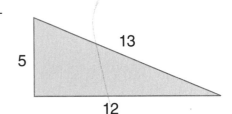

5

13

12

3. _____

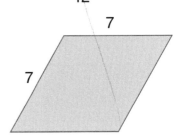

7

7

4. _____

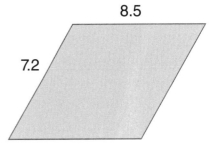

8.5

7.2

5. _____

4.5   3.2

3.2

Geography

South Asia

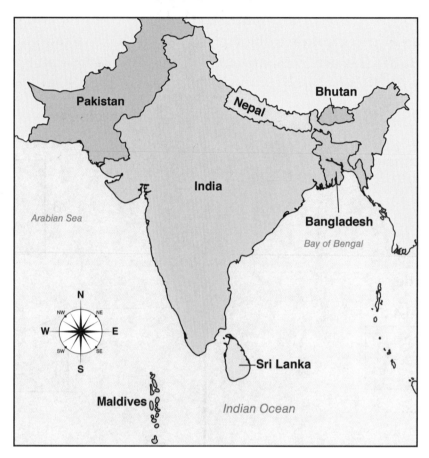

1. South Asia is made up of how many countries?   _____

2. Which country is both east and west of India?   _____

3. Which country is made up of many small islands?   _____

4. Which is the largest country in South Asia?   _____

5. Which two South Asian countries do not border the water?

   _____

6. The Arabian Sea borders the coast of which two mainland South Asian countries?

   _____

West of Greenwich   Longitude West of Greenwich

A   120°   B   150°   C   180°   D   150°   E   120°   F   90°

WEEK 4

Check off each box as you complete the day's work.

Spelling Words

amphibian

chieftain

coughing

efficient

fantasy

flexible

pamphlet

phenomenal

symphony

toughest

twelfth

typhoid

Get Creative!

Draw something you use to play your favorite sport.

A Memorable Moment

What sticks in your mind about this week? Write about it.

_____

_____

_____

_____

_____

_____

_____

Reading Record

	Book Title	Pages	Time
Monday			
Tuesday			
Wednesday			
Thursday			
Friday			

Describe a character you read about this week.

_____

_____

_____

_____

_____

_____

Read the article. Then answer the questions.

A Pyramid in Wyoming

When you think of pyramids, you probably picture one in Egypt or Mexico. Did you know that there is also a pyramid in the United States? Not many people are aware of it. You can find the pyramid, called the Ames Monument, off a quiet dirt road in the southeast corner of Wyoming.

Back in the 1800s, two brothers named Oliver and Oakes Ames worked with the Union Pacific Railroad to build train tracks that stretched across the country. This was a spectacular feat. However, Oakes was later charged with dishonest business practices, so the Ames brothers and the railroad company gained a bad reputation. After the Ames brothers died, the people who ran Union Pacific wanted to restore the company's public image. So they built a monument near Sherman, a quiet town at the highest point along the rail line. The builder used blocks of pink granite found in the area to construct the monument—a 60-foot pyramid. An artist added two 9-foot-tall carved portraits, one of each Ames brother.

At one time, train passengers traveling through the area could get off the train and view the pyramid up close. However, since then, the railroad tracks have been moved, and the town of Sherman no longer exists. Few people come to see the Ames Monument anymore, and the odd structure has fallen into disrepair. As a result, this pyramid may eventually vanish into history.

· ·

1. **According to the passage, why did Union Pacific build the pyramid?**

   Ⓐ to give passengers something to look at

   Ⓑ to improve the railroad's public image

   Ⓒ to impress the Ames brothers

   Ⓓ to compete with Egyptian pyramids

2. **Which of these was an effect of Oakes Ames being charged with dishonest business practices?**

   Ⓐ The Ames brothers moved to Sherman.

   Ⓑ People stopped taking the train.

   Ⓒ Union Pacific gained a bad reputation.

   Ⓓ An artist carved Oakes Ames's portrait.

3. **What was probably the reason for choosing Sherman as the site of the monument?**

   Ⓐ It was the highest point along the rail line.

   Ⓑ A lot of people lived there.

   Ⓒ The Ames brothers died there.

   Ⓓ Union Pacific headquarters was there.

4. **What is the most likely reason that few people visit the pyramid today?**

   Ⓐ Passenger trains no longer stop there.

   Ⓑ Union Pacific built a different monument.

   Ⓒ The Ames brothers died.

   Ⓓ The pyramid is in disrepair.

Write It Right

Rewrite each sentence and correct the errors.

1. arent their no cookies left asked robert

   _____

2. whos going to collect the five oclock male when its delivered

   _____

3. ive know idea what your talking about

   _____

4. i comed to sea you but you wasnt there

   _____

MATH TIME

Use the survey results to complete the circle graph and the key. Color each section of the graph a different color. Be sure the colors on your graph match the data and your key.

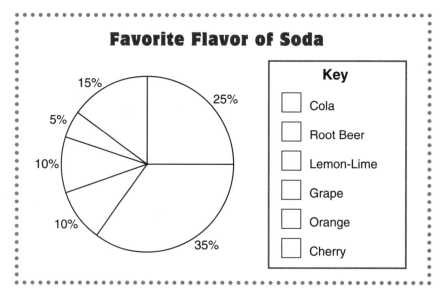

Survey Results

Cherry: 20 students

Cola: 70 students

Grape: 20 students

Lemon-Lime: 30 students

Orange: 10 students

Root Beer: 50 students

Favorite Flavor of Soda

15%
25%
5%
10%
10%
35%

Key

☐ Cola
☐ Root Beer
☐ Lemon-Lime
☐ Grape
☐ Orange
☐ Cherry

SPELL IT

The /f/ sound can be spelled several ways:

f   gh   ph   ff

Fill in the letter or letters that make the **/f/** sound in the spelling words for the week.
Then rewrite the word on the line next to it.

1. _____ enomenal   _____

2. chie _____ tain   _____

3. _____ lexible   _____

4. sym _____ ony   _____

5. am _____ ibian   _____

6. tou _____ est   _____

7. pam _____ let   _____

8. cou _____ ing   _____

9. twel _____ th   _____

10. _____ antasy   _____

11. e _____ icient   _____

12. ty _____ oid   _____

In My Own Words

Finish this story: *Max found the end of the rainbow, but there was no pot of gold.
Instead he found...*

LANGUAGE LINES

Write the clipped word that comes from each underlined word.

1. After class, Joe went back to his <u>dormitory</u>. _____

2. Mom has her final <u>examination</u> on Friday. _____

3. The scientist spends all day in her <u>laboratory</u>. _____

4. Chris's teacher found a <u>typographical error</u> in his report. _____

5. Esteban had to wear a <u>tuxedo</u> to the wedding. _____

6. The boss sent a <u>memorandum</u> about the meeting. _____

7. The college <u>graduate</u> applied for several jobs. _____

8. A <u>limousine</u> took the actor to the movie premiere. _____

MATH TIME

Solve the word problem about probability.

There is a bag with 18 colored marbles inside. There are 6 white marbles, 2 green marbles, 1 red marble, and 9 blue marbles. If one marble is selected at random, what is the probability that it will be one of the following colors?

1. green: _____   3. white: _____

2. blue: _____   4. red: _____

Read the story. Then answer the questions.

The First Fish

David and his grandfather had been fishing all day. Right before the sun went down, David finally felt a fish take the bait. "Gotcha!" he called out, reeling in his line.

David's grandfather watched his grandson struggle. He tipped open the cooler between him and David, where the eight fat fish the grandfather had caught earlier were placed on ice. "Easy now," he advised David. "You don't want to pull it in too fast."

Ignoring his grandfather, David jumped to his feet and cranked the reel as fast as he could.

"I can't let him get away! I've been waiting all day for this!"

Just when it seemed as if the fish would surface, David toppled backward onto the dock. The line had snapped, and it lay loosely coiled up across David's lap. His face fell.

"There goes my first fish," he mumbled sadly. His grandfather smiled knowingly. "It won't be your last," he said. "You'll bring in the next one."

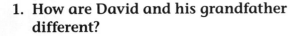

1. **How are David and his grandfather different?**

   Ⓐ David is calmer.

   Ⓑ David is less patient.

   Ⓒ David is better at fishing.

   Ⓓ David is less interested in fishing.

2. **What is the author's main purpose in writing the story?**

   Ⓐ to teach the value of listening to good advice

   Ⓑ to tell a story about how a boy and his grandfather become closer

   Ⓒ to explain the best techniques for catching fish

   Ⓓ to persuade people to go fishing

3. **What is one theme of the story?**

   Ⓐ Age brings experience and wisdom.

   Ⓑ Young people need to behave well.

   Ⓒ Fishing is an activity for older people.

   Ⓓ Honesty is important.

4. **What is the main idea of the last paragraph?**

   Ⓐ David should give up fishing.

   Ⓑ David should keep trying.

   Ⓒ David's grandfather plans to play a trick on David.

   Ⓓ People should forget about their own mistakes.

Vo·cab·u·lar·y

Many English words originally came from Greek and Latin **roots**. Roots are word parts that form the base of words and can give clues to the words' meanings.

terr = **land (territory)**

aqua/aqui = **water (aquarium)**

therm = **heat (thermos)**

chron = **time (chronological)**

Write each word from the box under its correct definition in the chart below. Use a dictionary if necessary.

territory	terrace	terrain	thermos
aquarium	aquifer	chronic	aquamarine
thermostat	chronicle	thermometer	chronology

terr	therm	aqua/aqui	chron
an area of land that belongs to someone or something:	measures someone's temperature:	a sea-like, blue-green color:	lasting for a long time, or repeatedly:
an outdoor sitting area:	a container to keep liquids warm or cold:	where fish live indoors:	a list of events arranged in time order:
the natural features of land or ground:	raises or lowers the heat in your home:	an underground layer of rock containing water:	the science of recording events by date:

LANGUAGE LINES

Circle the linking verb in each sentence. Write the predicate noun or predicate adjective on the line. The first one has been done for you.

1. Franklin (is) our hometown.   _hometown_

2. My mother's sisters are my aunts.   _____

3. Some family stories can be funny.   _____

4. The potato salad was quite delicious.   _____

5. The family reunion will be an important event.   _____

6. That spinach salad is bright green!   _____

7. I am so happy for the winner.   _____

8. Robin wishes Tony and Katie were her partners. _____

In My Own Words

Imagine that there is suddenly no gravity on Earth! Describe what you see happening around you.

Mind Jigglers

Shark Games

For each numbered clue, write the correct letter on the line at the bottom of the page. The letters will spell the answer to the shark joke.

1. What letter is in *SEAL* but not in *LAME*?

2. What letter is in *SWIPE* but not in *SPIES*?

3. What letter is in *TAIL* but not in *LIGHT*?

4. What letter is in *LAST* but not in *START*?

5. What letter is in *STALE* but not in *BEAST*?

6. What letter is in *NOTED* but not in *DENTED*?

7. What letter is in *DRAW* but not in *BRAID*?

8. What letter is in *LATER* but not in *REALLY*?

9. What letter is in *SEARCH* but not in *CREATES*?

10. What letter is in *SCARE* but not in *CRABS*?

11. What letter is in *COLD* but not in *DOCK*?

12. What letter is in *SHARE* but not in *BRASH*?

13. What letter is in *WATER* but not in *TWISTER*?

14. What letter is in *READ* but not in *SPEAR*?

15. What letter is in *MILE* but not in *SLIM*?

16. What letter is in *TIRE* but not in *BITE*?

What is a shark's favorite game?

$\overline{}_{1}$ $\overline{}_{2}$ $\overline{}_{3}$ $\overline{}_{4}$ $\overline{}_{5}$ $\overline{}_{6}$ $\overline{}_{7}$ $\overline{}_{8}$ $\overline{}_{9}$ $\overline{}_{10}$ $\overline{}_{11}$ $\overline{}_{12}$ $\overline{}_{13}$ $\overline{}_{14}$ $\overline{}_{15}$ $\overline{}_{16}$

MATH TIME

Least Common Multiple

To solve the riddle, find the Least Common Multiple (LCM) for each set of numbers. Then write the corresponding letter on the line above the LCM. The letters will spell out the solution to the riddle at the bottom of the page.

> **Remember:**
>
> The Least Common Multiple (LCM) of two or more numbers is the smallest multiple that the numbers have in common.
>
> **The LCM of 4 and 5 is 20.**
> **The LCM of 2 and 7 is 14.**

1. LCM of 2 and 4 = _____
   A

2. LCM of 5 and 6 = _____
   E

3. LCM of 3 and 4 = _____
   E

4. LCM of 4 and 5 = _____
   E

5. LCM of 6 and 9 = _____
   E

6. LCM of 5 and 3 = _____
   S

7. LCM of 7 and 3 = _____
   T

8. LCM of 22 and 4 = _____
   T

9. LCM of 16 and 3 = _____
   T

10. LCM of 6 and 8 = _____
    W

11. LCM of 10 and 8 = _____
    W

What did the bird buy at the mall?

___ ___ ___ ___ ___ ___   ___ ___ ___ ___ ___
 4   15 40 12 30 44   21 24 20 18 48

Geography

The Great Lakes

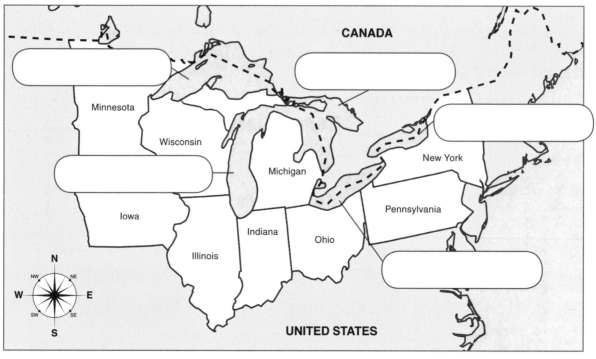

_____

_____

Use the clues below to label each of the five Great Lakes. Then write a caption for the map.

1. Lake Ontario is the farthest east.

2. Four states, including Wisconsin, border Lake Michigan.

3. Minnesota is bordered by Lake Superior to the northeast.

4. Lake Erie is south of Lake Huron.

5. Lake Huron is east of Lake Michigan.

WEEK 5

Check off each box as you complete the day's work.

☐ **ALL WEEK**

☐ **MONDAY**

☐ **TUESDAY**

☐ **WEDNESDAY**

☐ **THURSDAY**

☐ **FRIDAY**

Spelling Words

bilingual

binoculars

bipedal

centennial

centipede

semiannual

semicircle

triad

triathlon

triceps

unify

unique

Get Creative!

Draw a view of Earth from outer space.

A Memorable Moment

What sticks in your mind about this week? Write about it.

_____

_____

_____

_____

_____

_____

_____

Reading Record

	Book Title	Pages	Time
Monday			
Tuesday			
Wednesday			
Thursday			
Friday			

Describe a character you read about this week.

_____

_____

_____

_____

_____

_____

Read the story. Then answer the questions.

The Big Interview

Charles sat in the cafeteria with five other students, waiting for Ms. Swanson to interview all of them. Ms. Swanson, the seventh-grade science teacher, was looking for a lab helper. Charles's palms were sweaty and his face felt hot. He wondered if his face was red—and if anyone would notice.

As he prepared for his interview, Charles reviewed a set of index cards with notes that he had made earlier. On each card, he had written an answer to a question that Ms. Swanson might ask. "The emergency eyewash station is not a place to get a drink of water," he quietly read aloud from one card.

Charles decided to check out the other candidates. Nearby, a girl with dark red hair was shuffling her own set of index cards. He watched as she tore a card into tiny pieces and stuffed the pieces into her pocket. Suddenly she looked up at Charles. "Are you nervous?" she asked.

"No, I'm not nervous—not at all," Charles stammered. "What about you?"

"Uh, no, me neither," the girl responded.

At that moment, Ms. Swanson appeared. "Charles Locke?" she called out.

· ·

1. **What is the passage mostly about?**

   Ⓐ waiting to be interviewed

   Ⓑ working as a science teacher

   Ⓒ making notes on index cards

   Ⓓ a demanding science teacher

2. **What is most likely to happen next in the story?**

   Ⓐ Charles will talk to Ms. Swanson.

   Ⓑ Charles will tear up his index cards.

   Ⓒ Charles will help the girl prepare for her interview.

   Ⓓ Charles will decide not to try for the job.

3. **You can tell that the girl is nervous because _____.**

   Ⓐ her face turns red

   Ⓑ she tears up one of her index cards

   Ⓒ her palms are sweaty

   Ⓓ she reads her index cards

4. **The student who gets the job will be working _____.**

   Ⓐ in the cafeteria

   Ⓑ in the science lab

   Ⓒ in the library

   Ⓓ at the eyewash station

Write It Right

Rewrite each sentence and correct the errors.

1. brad make you're arms push thru the water shouted coach storm

   _____

2. I all ready finished doing the dishus mom said

   _____

3. wood you like some whipt cream with them berrys she asked

   _____

4. i likes the out fit that lupe was wering today

   _____

MATH TIME

Complete the decimal problems.

1. $2.0 + 3.5 =$ _____

2. $5.0 + 6.4 =$ _____

3. $2.3 + 4.0 =$ _____

4. $1.9 + 2.3 =$ _____

5. $3.4 + 9.7 =$ _____

6. $1.2 + 5.6 =$ _____

7. $5.2 - 4.1 =$ _____

8. $6.8 - 4.3 =$ _____

9. $8.7 - 2.1 =$ _____

10. $6.5 - 2.6 =$ _____

11. $4.6 - 0.9 =$ _____

12. $8.2 - 6.3 =$ _____

SPELL IT

> Some **prefixes** indicate numbers or amounts.
> **uni–:** one **bi–:** two **tri–:** three **semi–:** half or partial **cent–:** hundred

Complete the spelling words for the week by filling in the correct prefixes.

1. _____ **annual:** twice a year

2. _____ **ipede:** a creature with many legs (literally: hundred legs)

3. _____ **lingual:** speaking two languages

4. _____ **ad:** a group of three

5. _____ **fy:** to bring together as one

6. _____ **ennial:** a hundredth anniversary

7. _____ **pedal:** having two feet

8. _____ **athlon:** a three-part athletic event

9. _____ **que:** unlike any other; being the only one

10. _____ **ceps:** muscles with three points of attachment

11. _____ **circle:** half a circle

12. _____ **noculars:** using both eyes

In My Own Words

Use some of your spelling words to write a funny or factual sentence about a centipede.

LANGUAGE LINES

Comparative adjectives use –er to compare two people, places, things, or ideas.

Superlative adjectives use –est to compare three or more people, places, things, or ideas.

Circle the correct form of the adjective to complete each sentence. On the line, write *C* for comparative or *S* for superlative to identify the type of adjective.

1. The Rocky Mountains are _____ than the Appalachians.　　**taller**　　**tallest**

2. The Mississippi is the _____ river and the most famous.　　**mightier**　　**mightiest**

3. Chicago is the _____ city in the country, according to its nickname.　　**windier**　　**windiest**

4. I visited New York City, and it was _____ than where I live.　　**noisier**　　**noisiest**

5. Florida, the "Sunshine State," must be _____ than Illinois.　　**sunnier**　　**sunniest**

6. Alaska must be the _____ of all states, being so far north.　　**colder**　　**coldest**

7. Many places could claim to be the _____ in America.　　**prettier**　　**prettiest**

8. I would like to live in the place that is the _____.　　**friendlier**　　**friendliest**

MATH TIME

Solve the word problems about books.

1. Patricia bought a book at the bookstore. She got $2.25 from her mom, $3.25 from her dad, and $4.00 from her older sister to buy the book. Patricia had to kick in the last $2.49. How much did the book cost?

2. How much would Patricia's book cost if it were 25% off? Round to the nearest cent.

Answer: _____

Answer: _____

Read the article. Then answer the questions.

The Lone Tree

Many centuries ago, the Sahara was full of trees. The climate there was different from what it is now. As time passed, the land became dry and hot, and trees became scarce. But one acacia (uh-KAY-shuh) tree in the Ténéré (TAY-nay-RAY) region of Niger survived longer than the rest.

Caravans transporting goods across the vast expanse of desert used the Tree of Ténéré as a landmark. This tree was so important for navigating the sandy landscape that no one dared to cut off its branches for firewood. It was the only tree for almost 250 miles around.

In 1938, French military engineers dug a well near the tree. They discovered water more than 100 feet underground. That's how deep the roots of the acacia tree had reached to keep itself alive. Unfortunately, one of the military vehicles backed into the tree during the digging operation. The accident damaged one of the tree's main branches.

After World War II, trucks became the main form of transportation for caravans in the area, replacing camels. In 1973, the acacia tree was once again struck by a truck. This time the tree could not withstand the force. The remains of the world's loneliest tree were taken to the Niger National Museum. However, travelers still have a landmark to help them cross the desert. A metal monument now stands where the tree once grew.

· ·

1. **What happened as the weather changed in the Sahara?**

   Ⓐ Trucks replaced camels in caravans.

   Ⓑ Trees in the region died out.

   Ⓒ People stopped traveling through this area.

   Ⓓ Camels became more popular than trucks.

2. **What happened just before the first accident caused damage to the Tree of Ténéré?**

   Ⓐ French engineers started digging a well.

   Ⓑ A metal monument was built.

   Ⓒ The climate in the region changed.

   Ⓓ People cut off tree branches for firewood.

3. **What happened before the French dug a well near the tree?**

   Ⓐ Engineers found water far below ground.

   Ⓑ Remains of the tree were shipped to the Niger National Museum.

   Ⓒ People used the tree for navigation.

   Ⓓ A truck struck the tree.

4. **The Tree of Ténéré died _____.**

   Ⓐ many centuries ago

   Ⓑ in 1938

   Ⓒ in 1973

   Ⓓ before World War II

Vo·cab·u·lar·y

Synonyms are words that have almost the same meaning. For example, the words **complicated** and **complex** are synonyms.

This math puzzle is fairly complicated.

I hope I'll be able to solve this complex puzzle.

A. Use the words in the box to write a synonym for each word below. Use a dictionary if necessary.

remove	glossy	instruct	persuasive
conclude	humorous	bewilder	courageous

1. convincing _____

2. lustrous _____

3. confound _____

4. terminate _____

5. eliminate _____

6. witty _____

7. valiant _____

8. educate _____

B. Complete each sentence with a synonym from Activity A.

1. Let's _____ this lesson five minutes before lunchtime.
   (conclude)

2. I brushed my cat until her fur looked _____.
   (glossy)

3. This detergent will _____ stains from your clothing.
   (remove)

4. The _____ firefighter saved three people's lives.
   (courageous)

5. Complicated science projects often _____ me.
   (bewilder)

6. A _____ argument may change someone's mind.
   (persuasive)

LANGUAGE LINES

You can correct **run-on sentences** by turning them into two sentences or by forming a **compound** or a **complex sentence.**

> **Compound sentence:** Alejandro played soccer, and Lucas played baseball.
>
> **Complex sentence:** When James came home, he started his homework.

Correct and rewrite each run-on sentence as directed.

1. Patty and I went to the shoe store we tried on lots of shoes.

   Two simple sentences: _____

   _____

2. We went to the card store, I needed a birthday card.

   Complex sentence: _____

   _____

3. Patty likes to try on clothes, I would rather try on shoes.

   Compound sentence: _____

   _____

In My Own Words

Make a list of 10 words that describe you.

Mind Jigglers

Water Works

A. See how quickly you can answer the questions below.

1. Where are six places you could find water in nature?

_____ _____ _____

_____ _____ _____

2. What are six things that you can put in water?

_____ _____ _____

_____ _____ _____

3. What are six things that you can use water for?

_____ _____ _____

_____ _____ _____

B. Your body is 70 percent water. A cup of water weighs about half a pound. About how many cups of water do you have in your body?

Your weight: _____ pounds

Cups of water in your body: _____

C. There are 3 identical pitchers in a row. The first one has twice as much water in it as the third one. The second one has one-third the amount of water as the first one. Draw the amount of water in each pitcher.

MATH TIME

What's Your Range?

Remember:

Range is the difference between the greatest and the least number in a set of data.

> **Set: 21, 15, 27, 12, 20**
> 27 − 12 = 15
> **Range: 15**

Find the **range**.

1. 5, 7, 15, 8, 23, 8 _____

2. 59, 48, 61, 61, 57, 42, 60, 53, 54 _____

3. 23, 31, 45, 22, 62, 41, 26, 38 _____

Remember:

Mean is the average of a set of data. Add the numbers, then divide the sum of the numbers by the number of addends.

> **Set: 21, 15, 27, 12, 20**
> 21 + 15 + 27 + 12 + 20 = 95
> 95 ÷ 5 = 19
> **Mean: 19**

Find the **mean**.

1. 19, 3, 7, 22, 5, 25 _____

2. 13, 32, 6, 26, 30, 44, 12, 29 _____

3. 61, 46, 23, 40, 39, 21, 32, 28 _____

Remember:

Median is the middle number in a set of sequenced data.

> **Set: 21, 15, 27, 12, 20**
> 12, 15, 20, 21, 27
> **Median: 20**

Find the **median**.

1. 2, 6, 28, 9, 40, 9, 17 _____

2. 56, 36, 43, 52, 59, 20, 70 _____

3. 41, 19, 81, 80, 51, 57, 69, 15, 60 _____

Remember:

Mode is the number that appears the most often in a set of data. Some sets have no mode.

> **Set: 21, 15, 27, 12, 20**
> **There is no mode.**

Find the **mode**.

1. 22, 22, 22, 22 _____

2. 14, 12, 19, 13, 12, 13, 17, 12 _____

3. 33, 31, 45, 92, 47, 86 _____

Geography

Countries of Western Europe

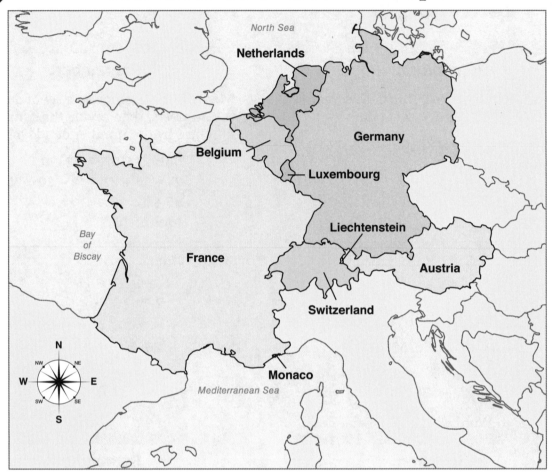

1. How many countries are in Western Europe? _____

2. Which sea is to the south of Western Europe? _____

3. Which country is bordered by both the Bay of Biscay and the Mediterranean Sea? _____

4. Liechtenstein is between which two countries? _____

5. Which countries border Luxembourg?

_____

6. What is the smallest country in Western Europe? _____

WEEK 6

Check off each box as you complete the day's work.

Spelling Words

beliefs

boundaries

echoes

halves

journeys

mosquitoes

passersby

schedules

substances

thieves

tomatoes

varieties

Get Creative!

Turn this line into a banana split.

A Memorable Moment

What sticks in your mind about this week? Write about it.

_____

_____

_____

_____

_____

_____

_____

Reading Record

	Book Title	Pages	Time
Monday			
Tuesday			
Wednesday			
Thursday			
Friday			

Describe a character you read about this week.

_____

_____

_____

_____

_____

_____

Read the story. Then answer the questions.

The Egg Drop

Marisol, Jack, and Ramon met after school to work on their group science project. Their assignment was to find a way to protect an egg from breaking as it was dropped from a two-story building. Marisol and Ramon were busy working with their materials, which included a pile of newspapers, some bubble wrap, and rubber bands. Marisol was tearing newspapers into strips and watching Jack doodle in a notebook. Finally, she couldn't stay quiet any longer.

"Jack, when are you going to help us?" she asked. "We need to get this project done today."

Ramon reached across the table for another rubber band to weave into the rubber mat he was trying to make. "Yeah, Jack," he said. "Could you put down your cartoons and help us?" Jack was a good friend, but he didn't seem to give science class the same attention that Ramon and Marisol did. His mind always seemed to be somewhere else—mainly in his notebook.

Jack looked up so slowly that Marisol and Ramon thought he may not have heard them at all. Then he turned the page toward them. Jack had sketched a diagram that showed an egg in the center of a layer of newspaper and bubble wrap. The egg had been wrapped with several rubber bands, which crisscrossed each other to make a thick layer of padding. Marisol and Ramon were impressed.

"I was just brainstorming," Jack said. "Do you think it'll work?"

. . . .

1. **What do the three students have in common?**

   Ⓐ They like to draw cartoons.

   Ⓑ They are working on the same project.

   Ⓒ They are easily distracted.

   Ⓓ They do not want to use rubber bands.

2. **How is Jack's way of working on the project different from that of his partners?**

   Ⓐ He doesn't work as hard as they do.

   Ⓑ He sketches his ideas first.

   Ⓒ He doesn't care if the egg breaks.

   Ⓓ He wants to spend more time on it.

3. **How is Jack's plan different from Ramon's?**

   Ⓐ It uses different materials.

   Ⓑ It will be more difficult to do.

   Ⓒ It will keep the egg from breaking.

   Ⓓ It uses rubber bands in a different way.

4. **What do Marisol and Ramon probably think at the end of the story?**

   Ⓐ They decide their ideas are not very good.

   Ⓑ They think they need a sketch to succeed.

   Ⓒ They agree they do not need Jack's help.

   Ⓓ They realize Jack has been working the whole time.

Write It Right

Rewrite each sentence and correct the errors.

1. josh torie and maddie went to disney world

   _____

   _____

2. they road on three rides called space mountain rock 'n' roller coaster and test track

   _____

   _____

3. theyre favorite part were watching the firework's at epcot center

   _____

   _____

MATH TIME

Solve the multiplication and division problems.

1. $2.2 \times 3.0 =$ _____

2. $8.6 \times 2.0 =$ _____

3. $1.0 \times 5.3 =$ _____

4. $5.0 \times 2.3 =$ _____

5. $6.9 \times 6.5 =$ _____

6. $10.25 \times 11.3 =$ _____

7. $9.1 \div 7.0 =$ _____

8. $4.5 \div 1.8 =$ _____

9. $5.39 \div 1.1 =$ _____

10. $23.0 \div 5.0 =$ _____

11. $17.836 \div 3.43 =$ _____

12. $12.015 \div 1.5 =$ _____

SPELL IT

Most plural nouns are formed by adding **–s** or **–es**. Sometimes you must also change the last letter of the singular noun before adding **–s** or **–es**.

Change each singular noun to its plural form to make the spelling words for the week.

1. half _____

2. variety _____

3. boundary _____

4. journey _____

5. belief _____

6. passerby _____

7. echo _____

8. schedule _____

9. thief _____

10. substance _____

11. tomato _____

12. mosquito _____

In My Own Words

An example of a tongue twister is "Sister Susie sells seashells by the seashore." Write two of your own tongue twisters.

LANGUAGE LINES

The present progressive tense of a verb shows that an action is in progress. The action is happening now and will continue for a period of time.

Underline the present progressive verb in each sentence. The first one has been done for you.

1. Shoppers <u>are waiting</u> for the store to open.

2. The manager is unlocking the door.

3. Everyone is hoping for a bargain.

4. I am searching for shoes for the party.

5. Chris is unfolding a green sweater.

6. My parents are paying for these shoes.

MATH TIME

Complete the table below so that each row shows three representations of the same value. The first row has been done for you.

Fraction	Decimal	Percent
$\frac{1}{4}$	0.25	25%
		50%
$\frac{7}{10}$		
		75%
	0.8	
$\frac{2}{5}$		

Read the article. Then answer the questions.

The Loneliest Island

In the middle of the frigid South Atlantic Ocean, one island stands alone. It lies near Antarctica. But it is far enough away that early explorers had difficulty finding it. At about four miles long, the island is covered with glaciers. It is home to an inactive volcano and huge amounts of ice. The island is cold year-round, with an average temperature of about 29°F. The steep cliffs that surround the island make sea landings almost impossible. This is Bouvet Island, the loneliest island in the world.

A French explorer discovered Bouvet Island in 1739, but the island was so difficult to approach that nobody set foot on it for nearly a hundred years. No people live on Bouvet Island, and little vegetation grows there. Seals come and go, but they haven't seen humans since the mid- to late-20th century, when seal hunting and whaling stopped in the area.

In recent years, Bouvet Island has had a little more contact with the world. Norway, which claimed the island in 1928, set up an unmanned weather station there in 1977. Today, this quiet island near the South Pole sends weather data to a satellite, which transmits the information to researchers in Norway. Scientists learn more every day about the island and its surroundings. Meanwhile, Bouvet Island stands strong and silent in the harsh climate.

. . . .

1. **What could you correctly predict from the title of the article?**

    Ⓐ The island is very small.

    Ⓑ No one lives on the island.

    Ⓒ The passage is about Antarctica.

    Ⓓ Only lonely people live on the island.

2. **What could you correctly predict about Bouvet Island after reading the first sentence?**

    Ⓐ It is cold most of the year.

    Ⓑ It is volcanic.

    Ⓒ Norway claimed it in 1928.

    Ⓓ It is near the North Pole.

3. **What can you conclude after reading that steep cliffs surround the island?**

    Ⓐ The island is covered in glaciers.

    Ⓑ Explorers cannot find the island.

    Ⓒ There is nowhere to dock a boat on the island.

    Ⓓ The island is near the South Pole.

4. **After scientists receive data from the weather station, they will most likely _____.**

    Ⓐ try to determine the island's location

    Ⓑ study weather patterns on the island

    Ⓒ track the movements of seals

    Ⓓ send the information to a satellite

Vo·cab·u·lar·y

Antonyms are words that have opposite meanings.

> **Doubt** is an antonym of **certainty**.
>
> **Knowledge** is an antonym of **ignorance**.

Write each word from the box under its correct antonym in the grid to complete a row, column, or diagonal. Circle the winning four-in-a-row. Use a dictionary if necessary.

| deny | active | insult | definite |
| humble | flexible | opponent | taper |

lively	sure	compliment	teammate
_____	_____	_____	_____
immature	vague	rigid	confirm
_____	_____	_____	_____
limber	modest	refuse	arrogant
_____	_____	_____	_____
offend	widen	tragic	idle
_____	_____	_____	_____

LANGUAGE LINES

An adverb can modify a verb, an adjective, or another adverb.
Adverbs can tell where, how, when, and to what extent.

Underline the adverb and draw an arrow to the word it modifies. The first one has been done for you.

1. "There you are!" cried Alex's mother.

2. His mother anxiously asked him where he'd been.

3. "I missed the bus and had to walk here," Alex replied.

4. "You have an orthodontist appointment tomorrow," Alex's mother said.

5. "That means you have to leave school early," she continued.

6. "I'll be very happy when my braces are removed," Alex said.

7. "Me, too," his mother replied tiredly.

In My Own Words

Make a list of five of your favorite activities and explain why you like them.

Mind Jigglers

Hink Pinks and Hinky Pinkies

A. Write two rhyming words to match each description. For example, a healthy chime is a well bell, and a thorny little instrument is a thistle whistle.

ill baby chicken _____

chubby kitty _____

rodent dwelling _____

shark's plate _____

bloody tale _____

rabbit seat _____

idle flower _____

wet puppy _____

grumpy taxi driver _____

timid bug _____

intelligent graph _____

unkind adolescent _____

bad breakfast item _____

funny female horse _____

phony serpent _____

frightening pet bird _____

monster university _____

upbeat Thanksgiving bird _____

reptilian magician _____

B. Now make up some of your own.

_____

_____

_____

_____

_____

_____

_____

MATH TIME

Outer Planets

What are the planets Jupiter, Saturn, Uranus, and Neptune called? To find the answer to this question, solve each problem on the right. Then write the corresponding letter on the line above the correct number. The letters will spell out the answer.

exponent
↓
2^2
↑
base

The large number is called a *base*. The small number is called an *exponent*. It shows how many times the base is used as a factor.

5^2 is read as "five squared."
It tells you to multiply 5 by itself two times.
$$5 \times 5 = 25$$

4^3 is read as 4 "cubed."
It tells you to multiply 4 by itself three times.
$$4 \times 4 \times 4 = 64$$

2^5 is read as "two to the fifth power."
It tells you to multiply 2 by itself five times.
$$2 \times 2 \times 2 \times 2 \times 2 = 32$$

A $4^2 =$ _____

A $8^2 =$ _____

G $6^2 =$ _____

G $3^3 =$ _____

I $5^3 =$ _____

N $5^2 =$ _____

S $9^2 =$ _____

S $7^2 =$ _____

T $2^7 =$ _____

___ ___ ___
36   64   81

___ ___ ___ ___ ___ ___
27   125   16   25   128   49

Geography

Capital Cities of South America

1. What is the capital of Brazil? _____

2. What is the capital of Argentina? _____

3. Bogotá is the capital of which country? _____

4. Montevideo is the capital of which country? _____

5. The capital cities of three South American countries are located on the northern coast of the continent. Name the countries and their capitals.

_____

_____

WEEK 7

Check off each box as you complete the day's work.

☐ **ALL WEEK**

☐ **MONDAY**

☐ **TUESDAY**

☐ **WEDNESDAY**

☐ **THURSDAY**

☐ **FRIDAY**

Spelling Words

acceptable

committee

embarrass

exaggerate

exceed

interrupt

occasion

occurrence

opportunity

parallel

profession

recommend

Get Creative!

Draw what you think the inside of your locker will look like next year.

A Memorable Moment

What sticks in your mind about this week? Write about it.

_____

_____

_____

_____

_____

_____

_____

Reading Record

	Book Title	Pages	Time
Monday	_____	_____	_____
Tuesday	_____	_____	_____
Wednesday	_____	_____	_____
Thursday	_____	_____	_____
Friday	_____	_____	_____

Describe a character you read about this week.

_____

_____

_____

_____

_____

_____

Read the story. Then answer the questions.

Moving Day

Gina, Julius, and Eddy sat on Uncle Tim's living room floor. Uncle Tim was moving across town, and the kids were trying to decide how to work together to pack their uncle's books.

"Julius, you can start putting the books into boxes," Gina directed.

"No," Julius argued. "I think Eddy should do that. I'm the strongest, so it's best if I carry the boxes to the truck after Eddy has packed them."

"I don't want to pack them," grumbled Eddy. "I want to watch TV."

"Too bad, Eddy," said Gina. "Your job is to put the books into the boxes. Then I'll tape the boxes shut, and Julius will carry them out."

"I have a better idea," Eddy declared.

"Eddy!" Gina and Julius both said as they stood up, annoyed with their brother. "We know you want to watch TV," Gina said, "but Uncle Tim needs your help today."

"I *know*!" Eddy responded. "I want to help. How about if you put the books into the boxes and I close the boxes—but not with tape?" Eddy then dragged a box of books to the center of the living room. He folded down the flaps on the top of the box in clockwise order and finished by tucking half of the last one under the first one. Then he tipped the box over on its side. The flaps stayed shut, and nothing fell out. "See?" Eddy exclaimed.

Gina crossed her arms and raised her eyebrows. "Fine. I guess I'll pack, then," she said.

Eddy smiled. He clicked the TV remote and waited for his sister to finish filling a box.

. . . .

1. **Which statement does the passage support?**

   Ⓐ Julius, Gina, and Eddy cannot find a way to work together.

   Ⓑ Eddy is more excited to help Uncle Tim than Gina is.

   Ⓒ Julius is more eager to carry the boxes than Gina is.

   Ⓓ Uncle Tim has a better TV than the kids do.

2. **Gina and Julius are both _____.**

   Ⓐ reading Uncle Tim's books

   Ⓑ ready to watch TV instead of work

   Ⓒ good at giving orders

   Ⓓ eager to carry the boxes

3. **What *cannot* be concluded from the passage?**

   Ⓐ The kids want to help their uncle.

   Ⓑ Everyone wants to pack the boxes.

   Ⓒ Eddy is clever.

   Ⓓ Julius is strong.

4. **Why is Eddy smiling at the end of the story?**

   Ⓐ He can watch TV while Gina fills the boxes.

   Ⓑ He can watch TV instead of helping.

   Ⓒ He likes his uncle's books.

   Ⓓ He is glad that he does not have to use tape.

Write It Right

Rewrite each sentence and correct the errors.

1. keli and glen want two go horse back riding on friday at three o clock

_____

_____

2. the smith twins sara and emily always where matching outfits wearever they go

_____

_____

3. its all most lunch time shouted simon from the top of the stares

_____

_____

MATH TIME

Find the volume of each shape below by multiplying the length by the height by the width.

1. _____

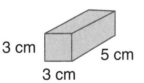

3 cm   5 cm
3 cm

2. _____

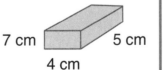

7 cm   5 cm
4 cm

3. _____

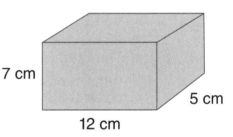

7 cm   5 cm
12 cm

4. _____

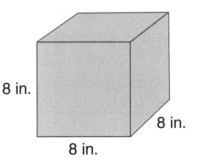

8 in.   8 in.
8 in.

SPELL IT

> Some words have **double consonants** and **double vowels**.

Fill in the missing double letters to make the spelling words for the week.

1. emba _____ a _____

2. o _____ ortunity

3. reco _____ end

4. a _____ eptable

5. commi _____ _____

6. o _____ u _____ ence

7. o _____ asion

8. exa _____ erate

9. inte _____ upt

10. para _____ el

11. profe _____ ion

12. exc _____ d

In My Own Words

Finish this story starter: *Kelly had always wanted a cat, but there was something strange about the little kitten sitting on her doorstep.*

LANGUAGE LINES

A **clause** is a group of related words that has its own subject and predicate.
An **independent clause** can stand alone as a complete sentence,
while a **dependent clause** cannot.

Circle whether the underlined group of words is an *independent clause* or a *dependent clause*.

1. Because birds are popular, pet stores carry a variety of them.   **independent   dependent**

2. They are popular because they are colorful and smart.   **independent   dependent**

3. I love my canary because of its yellow feathers.   **independent   dependent**

4. He sings when I uncover the cage in the morning.   **independent   dependent**

5. I bought my bird at the pet store in the mall.   **independent   dependent**

6. When he needs to eat, I fill his cup with seeds.   **independent   dependent**

MATH TIME

Look at each value in the box. Locate the value on the number line and write the corresponding letter above the line. The letters will spell out the solution to the riddle.

What goes up when rain comes down?

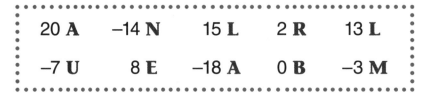

| 20 **A** | −14 **N** | 15 **L** | 2 **R** | 13 **L** |
| −7 **U** | 8 **E** | −18 **A** | 0 **B** | −3 **M** |

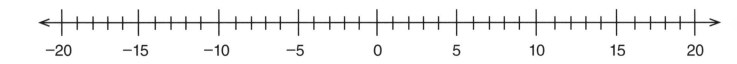

−20   −15   −10   −5   0   5   10   15   20

Read the article. Then answer the questions.

The Famous Rockettes

Imagine a long line of dancers performing a difficult high kick at exactly the same time. That was the vision of Russell Markert, who came up with the idea for the Rockettes back in 1925. The Rockettes, an all-female dance group, have come a long way with their high kicks. They have performed at Radio City Music Hall in New York City since its opening in 1932.

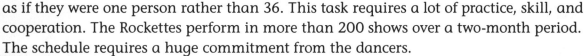

The goal of the Rockettes is for all of the dancers to make the same movements at the exact same time, as if they were one person rather than 36. This task requires a lot of practice, skill, and cooperation. The Rockettes perform in more than 200 shows over a two-month period. The schedule requires a huge commitment from the dancers.

Over the years, more than 3,000 women have danced as Rockettes. They say that performing with the group is a dream come true, despite the long hours of practice and the demanding schedule. They love it when the audience stands and cheers.

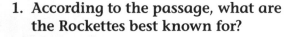

1. **According to the passage, what are the Rockettes best known for?**

   Ⓐ their individual dance skills

   Ⓑ their training with Russell Markert

   Ⓒ their high kicks

   Ⓓ their demanding schedule

2. **Based on the passage, who was Russell Markert?**

   Ⓐ a member of the audience

   Ⓑ the founder of the Rockettes

   Ⓒ the first male dancer in the Rockettes

   Ⓓ the owner of Radio City Music Hall

3. **Which theme does the passage communicate?**

   Ⓐ Dance is a good form of exercise.

   Ⓑ Female and male dancers are different.

   Ⓒ Many dancers can perform together as if they are one.

   Ⓓ Dance has changed over time.

4. **Based on the passage, what conclusion can you draw about the Rockettes?**

   Ⓐ It is easy to become a Rockette.

   Ⓑ Men have recently joined the group.

   Ⓒ They are popular with audiences today.

   Ⓓ They were more popular in the past.

Vo·cab·u·lar·y

A **prefix** is a word part that comes at the beginning of a word and affects its meaning.

The prefixes **em–** and **en–** mean "in" or "into."

The prefix **inter–** means "between."

The prefix **trans–** means "across."

A. Add the prefix **em–**, **en–**, **inter–**, or **trans–** to each word or word part in the box. The words you form will answer the clues below. Write the words next to the correct clues. Use a dictionary if necessary.

_____ brace   _____ vene   _____ danger   _____ courage

_____ mit   _____ portation   _____ mission   _____ continental

1. something that can carry you across distances   _____

2. something between two acts in a play   _____

3. to take someone into your arms   _____

4. to send a message across a distance   _____

5. to put in harm's way   _____

6. to give support and confidence   _____

7. between two or more countries   _____

8. to come between two people   _____

B. Use at least two of the words from Activity A in a sentence.

_____

_____

_____

LANGUAGE LINES

A **prepositional phrase** is a group of words that begins with a preposition and ends with a noun or pronoun. This noun or pronoun is called the **object** of the preposition.

Write the prepositional phrase from the box to complete each sentence. Circle the preposition. Then draw a line under the object of the preposition.

around the room	during the meal	to the dinner	at school
after the messy diners	for our class trip	onto warm plates	

1. The sixth grade had a spaghetti dinner _____.

2. We wanted to raise money _____.

3. About 60 people came _____.

4. We put up twinkling lights _____ so it would look special.

5. We played music _____ to be festive.

6. Some students' job was to dish out the spaghetti _____.

7. Other students cleared the tables and cleaned up _____.

In My Own Words

What is the most important attribute of a friend? Why is this important to you?

Mind Jigglers

School Lunch

A. All of the children listed below are very picky about the lunches they eat at school. All of the items in each child's lunch must start with the same letter as his or her name. Fill in the chart to make each child a lunch.

Name	Main Dish	Fruit or Veggie	Snack or Dessert	Drink
Sarah				
Pete				
Carlos				
Trina				
Michael				
Fiona				
Gina				

B. Garret and Jennifer both have double letters in their names. Can you make a different lunch for each kid, using only foods with double letters?

Name	Main Dish	Fruit or Veggie	Snack or Dessert	Drink
Garrett				
Jennifer				

MATH TIME

New Deli Directions

The letters on the grid below represent different buildings in the town of New Deli.
Use the grid to answer the questions.

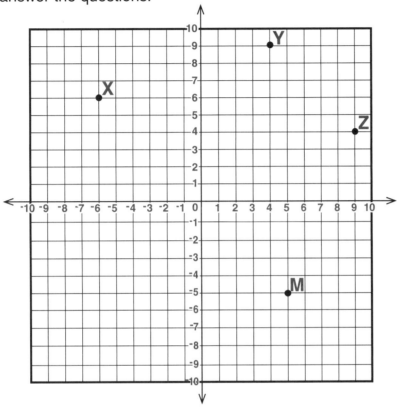

1. If *X* is the town's grocery store, what is the ordered pair for that location? _____

2. The City Bank is located at (9, 4) and the Town Food Court is located
   at (4, 9). Which letter represents each business?

   _____

3. If *M* is the New Deli School, what is the ordered pair for that location? _____

4. Patrick lives at the intersection of (–2, –4) and Whitney lives at the
   intersection of (6, –8). Plot each of their homes on the map and label
   Patrick's house *P* and Whitney's house *W*.

5. If a square represents one block, how many blocks must Patrick _____
   walk to get to Whitney's house without traveling diagonally?

Geography

Landscape of Asia

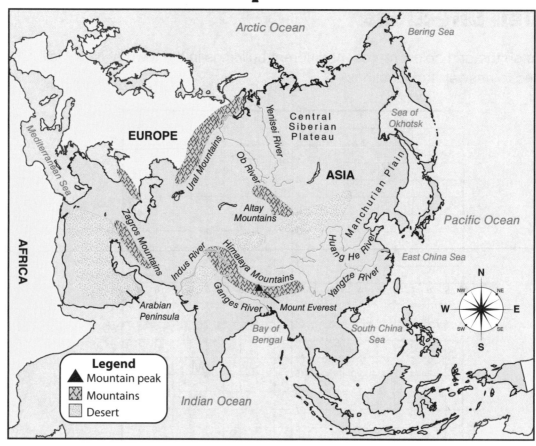

1. Which desert is between the Altay Mountains and the Manchurian Plain? _____

2. Which mountain range is the main division between Asia and Europe? _____

3. What is the name of the landform that is east of the Yenisei River? _____

4. In which direction are the Himalayas from the Zagros Mountains, southeast or southwest? _____

5. Which river is directly north of the Yangtze River? _____

6. Which landform covers the Arabian Peninsula? _____

West of Greenwich   Longitude West of Greenwich

A   120°   B   150°   C   180°   D   150°   E   120°   F   90°

WEEK 8

Check off each box as you complete the day's work.

Spelling Words

castle

chalkboard

condemn

doorknob

doubtful

exhaustion

honorable

plumber

pneumonia

shipwreck

signpost

wholesome

Get Creative!

Turn this scribble into a duck.

A Memorable Moment

What sticks in your mind about this week? Write about it.

_____

_____

_____

_____

_____

_____

_____

Reading Record

	Book Title	Pages	Time
Monday	_____	_____	_____
Tuesday	_____	_____	_____
Wednesday	_____	_____	_____
Thursday	_____	_____	_____
Friday	_____	_____	_____

Describe a character you read about this week.

_____

_____

_____

_____

_____

Read the article. Then answer the questions.

Flowers for Dinner

Flowers might look pretty on the dinner table. But what about serving them for dinner? In many cultures all around the world, people eat and enjoy a variety of flowers in their food.

The purple flowers of the lavender plant add a sweet lemon taste to chocolate cake or ice cream. Pansies, which have a grassy flavor, are a delicious addition to green salads. Bright yellow dandelion petals look cheerful when sprinkled over rice. Squash blossoms can be fried or stuffed with cheese. And the flowers of plants such as jasmine and chamomile are commonly used to make tea.

Does snacking on flowers sound weird? You may have eaten flowers already without realizing it. Several vegetables, such as cauliflower and broccoli, are actually flower buds. Artichokes, if left on their stalks, form fuzzy purple blooms. And asparagus tips open into small, pale green or white flowers.

If you're interested in eating flowers, be sure to learn about the plants first. Not every flower is safe to eat. The best way to find a tasty—and safe—flower is to visit your local grocery store.

. . . .

1. **How are broccoli and lavender similar?**

   Ⓐ Both have a lemon taste.

   Ⓑ Both are flowering plants.

   Ⓒ Both are used for tea.

   Ⓓ Both have purple flowers.

2. **Why should you learn about a plant before eating its flower?**

   Ⓐ to make sure the flower is safe to eat

   Ⓑ to find out how to serve the flower

   Ⓒ to learn more about other cultures

   Ⓓ to find out how the flower tastes

3. **What is the main idea of the third paragraph?**

   Ⓐ Eating flowers is weird.

   Ⓑ Plants produce flowers of different colors.

   Ⓒ Some vegetables are flower buds.

   Ⓓ The flowers of some plants are used for teas.

4. **What is the main idea of the passage?**

   Ⓐ Many flowers can be eaten.

   Ⓑ Flowers are often eaten with desserts.

   Ⓒ Many people eat flowers without realizing it.

   Ⓓ Flowers are tastier than vegetables.

Write It Right

Rewrite each sentence and correct the errors.

1. we read the declaration of independence in hour class

   _____

2. nashville tennessee is the capitol of that state

   _____

3. a trip to the museum of natural history is a reel treet

   _____

4. josh asked can you come with me to the libary tomorrow

   _____

MATH TIME

Complete the order of operations problems. Do the problem inside the parentheses first. Next, do multiplication and division from left to right. Then do addition and subtraction from left to right.

1. 9 x (5 + 3) = _____72_____

2. 6 ÷ (6 − 3) = _____

3. 15 − (10 ÷ 2) = _____

4. 25 ÷ (10 − 5) = _____

5. 4 x 5 − (6 ÷ 2) = _____

6. 4 x (5 + 6) ÷ 2 = _____

7. 17 − 2 x (5 − 3) = _____

8. 16 x (4 x 2) = _____

9. 18 ÷ 9 + (6 ÷ 3) = _____

10. 3 + (6 + 3 − 5) ÷ 2 = _____

11. 45 − (5 x 5 + 10) = _____

12. 16 + (90 ÷ 5) = _____

> **Silent consonants** are letters in a word that are not pronounced when the word is spoken.

Circle the silent letters in the spelling words for the week. Then write each word and draw a line between its syllables. Use a dictionary to help you if necessary. The first one has been done for you.

1. plum(b)er _____plumb|er_____

2. signpost _____

3. chalkboard _____

4. shipwreck _____

5. condemn _____

6. castle _____

7. exhaustion _____

8. pneumonia _____

9. doubtful _____

10. doorknob _____

11. wholesome _____

12. honorable _____

In My Own Words

Invent an unusual new sandwich to be served at the school cafeteria. Name all the ingredients and explain how to prepare the sandwich.

LANGUAGE LINES

A prefix is a word part that comes before a base word and changes the meaning of the word. The prefixes in–, im–, il–, and de– mean "not" or "opposite of."

Complete each word with the correct prefix. Use a dictionary if necessary.

1. A person who is not active is _____active.

2. If you remove the value from something, you _____value it.

3. An act that is not legal is _____legal.

4. A person who is not mature is _____mature.

5. Something that is the opposite of activated is _____activated.

6. A person who is not patient is _____ patient.

MATH TIME

A. Find the area of the circles. The first one has been done for you.

$$A = \pi \times r^2$$
(area = 3.14 x radius²)

1. $r = 3$

   $A = \pi \times r^2$
   $A = 3.14 \times (3 \times 3)$

   $\underline{A = 28.26}$

2. $r = 4$

   _____

3. $r = 6$

   _____

B. Find the circumference. The first one has been done for you.

C = π x d (circumference = 3.14 x diameter) **or**
C = 2 x π x r (circumference = 2 x 3.14 x radius)

1. $d = 16$

   $C = \pi \times d$
   $C = 3.14 \times 16$

   $\underline{C = 50.24}$

2. $r = 4$

3. 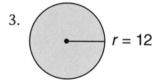 $r = 12$

   _____

4. $d = 20$

   _____

Read the story. Then answer the questions.

Disturbing the Peace

It was a beautiful spring morning on Lake Powell. Birds chirped and the trees rustled in the chilly morning breeze. Gentle waves moved across the surface of the clear blue water. Emma sat on the dock with her history book in her lap, occasionally looking out at the peaceful lake.

Suddenly, running footsteps came from behind, and a voice shouted, "Kowabunga!"

Before Emma could move an inch, her best friend Martha jumped directly over her head. Martha was shrieking with laughter as she jumped into the water. The cold water splashed all over Emma and soaked her.

As Martha swam back to the dock, Emma was wiping her face. "You said you'd never do that again!" Emma declared.

Martha pushed the hair out of her eyes and shrugged. "I said I wouldn't splash you at the pool, Em. We're at a lake now. And, come on, how much studying do you need to do on this trip? You've been reading all morning." Martha splashed the water playfully. "Come on, jump in! The water's great."

Emma sighed and closed her book. She would have to learn about pioneers along the Oregon Trail another day. The cool spring air was giving way to the summer sun. And besides, her best friend was just begging to be beaten in a race across the lake.

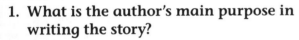

1. **What is the author's main purpose in writing the story?**

   Ⓐ to persuade people to read history books

   Ⓑ to tell a realistic story about friends

   Ⓒ to demonstrate how to swim in a lake

   Ⓓ to inform people about Lake Powell

2. **Why does the author describe the setting in the first paragraph?**

   Ⓐ to create a peaceful mood

   Ⓑ to show the main character's problem

   Ⓒ to establish a mystery

   Ⓓ to encourage readers to like Emma

3. **What does the author want you to think about Martha?**

   Ⓐ that she is careful and considerate

   Ⓑ that she is nicer than Emma

   Ⓒ that she is more playful than Emma

   Ⓓ that she is angry and bored

4. **The purpose of the last paragraph is to show that Emma _____.**

   Ⓐ will join Martha in the lake

   Ⓑ will continue reading her book

   Ⓒ is annoyed with Martha's splashing

   Ⓓ does not like to swim

Vo·cab·u·lar·y

A **suffix** is an ending added to a word or root that affects the word's meaning.

–ous, –ious: full of or possessing qualities of ➞ **nervous**: full of nerves or anxiety

–al, –ial: relating to ➞ **royal**: relating to kings and queens

–ic, ical: relating to ➞ **electric**: relating to electricity

A. Write the letter of the word that matches each definition. You will use the letters in Activity B.

_____ 1. full of nutrients

C. nutritous   B. nutrical
O. nutritious   F. nutrial

_____ 2. relating to nature

S. natural   N. naturous
G. naturial   A. naturical

_____ 3. relating to history

I. historal   K. histrious
R. historial   U. historical

_____ 4. full of wonder

W. wonderious   M. wonderal
P. wondrical   O. wondrous

_____ 5. relating to buying
and selling

T. commercic   Y. commercial
L. commercical   D. commercious

_____ 6. relating to comedy

J. comic   C. comedial
V. comedious   H. comedous

B. Unscramble the letters you wrote in Activity A to spell a word that means "full of happiness." Circle the word's suffix.

_____

C. Write a sentence using the word you spelled in Activity B.

_____

LANGUAGE LINES

A **complex sentence** contains one independent clause and one or more dependent clauses. Both clauses have a subject and a predicate, but dependent clauses do not express a complete thought.

In each complex sentence, draw one line under the dependent clause and two lines under the independent clause.

1. When a big snowstorm is predicted, we make a special trip to the grocery store.

2. The store is crowded because everyone has heard the weather forecast.

3. As my mom and dad shop for important supplies, I look for marshmallows.

4. Marshmallows and hot chocolate make a nice treat when you are snowed in.

5. If the electricity goes off, we will need flashlights and candles.

6. Unless the weather forecast is wrong, we will not have school the next day.

7. I like to help build a fire in the fireplace when there is a big storm.

8. We toast marshmallows in the fire until we go to bed.

In My Own Words

Describe an exciting experience you've recently had. Where were you? Who were you with? Include specific details about what happened.

Mind Jigglers

Spoonerisms

A. A *spoonerism* is a short phrase in which the initial sounds of the words have been switched, often with a humorous result. Find each spoonerism in the story and write the phrase correctly. The first one has been done for you.

One day, Timmy and his ~~sittle lister~~ *little sister* went to the playground. Timmy climbed up a lig badder

to go down the sleep stide. Then he and his sister hug a dole in the sandbox. After that, Timmy

climbed to the top of the bonkey mars and slid down the pall tole. On the hay wome, Timmy

and his sister bopped sty the puck dond. They saw a dommy muck with her dellow yucklings.

· ·

B. Think of a spoonerism for each phrase. Then use it in a sentence.

water bottle _____

grilled cheese _____

math book _____

bubble gum _____

bake cookies _____

take a shower _____

Challenge: Write a sentence containing two spoonerisms that are not already on this page.

_____

_____

MATH TIME

Box and Whisker Plot

Olivia collected the following data about her classmates and their scores on the last spelling test:

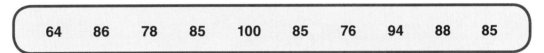

| 64 | 86 | 78 | 85 | 100 | 85 | 76 | 94 | 88 | 85 |

She put the data into a graph called a Box and Whisker Plot. The graph looked like this:

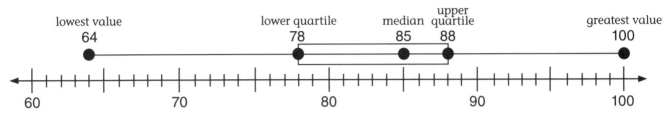

Now it's your turn. Follow the directions below to construct a Box and Whisker Plot for the data in the box, which shows the scores that Olivia's classmates received on their last math test.

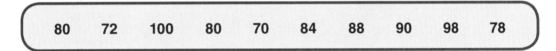

| 80 | 72 | 100 | 80 | 70 | 84 | 88 | 90 | 98 | 78 |

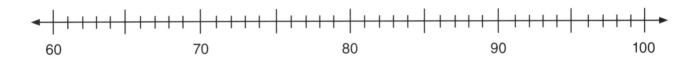

1. Write the scores on this line, from least to greatest value on the graph.

_____

2. Draw dots to show the lowest value and the greatest value above the graph. Draw a line connecting the dots.

3. Draw a dot and label the median score. (When there is an even amount of numbers in a data set, take the average of the two numbers in the middle to find the median.)

4. Draw a dot and label the median of the lower range of the scores.

5. Draw a dot and label the median of the upper range of the scores.

6. Draw a box around the three median values.

Geography

Countries of North America

1. Which large island belongs to Denmark? _____

2. Which country is west of the Atlantic Ocean, east of the _____
   Pacific Ocean, and directly north of the Gulf of Mexico?

3. Which country does the Hudson Bay border? _____

4. Which two Central American countries border Mexico to the south?

   _____

5. Which two Caribbean countries share an island?

   _____

WEEK 9

Check off each box as you complete the day's work.

Spelling Words

assistance

assistants

complement

compliment

finally

finely

foreword

forward

patience

patients

stationary

stationery

Get Creative!

Draw your favorite beverage, and write a caption telling what it is.

A Memorable Moment

What sticks in your mind about this week? Write about it.

_____

_____

_____

_____

_____

_____

_____

Reading Record

	Book Title	Pages	Time
Monday	_____	_____	_____
Tuesday	_____	_____	_____
Wednesday	_____	_____	_____
Thursday	_____	_____	_____
Friday	_____	_____	_____

Describe a character you read about this week.

_____

_____

_____

_____

_____

_____

Read the article. Then answer the questions.

A Sheltered Life

If you visit the animal shelter in Salinas, California, you'll see giant wooden cutouts of a dog and a cat. These signs were placed in front of the building to catch people's attention. The supersized cutouts make people curious and encourage them to visit the shelter—and maybe even adopt a pet. Each year, the Salinas shelter takes in about 2,000 dogs and 2,000 cats. The animals are either strays or are dropped off by people who couldn't take care of them. Of the 4,000 animals, some of them are eventually adopted into new homes. Some animals are transferred to other shelters. And, unfortunately, some cannot be saved because they are too sick or are considered dangerous.

Animal shelters provide food, medicine, and a safe place for animals to sleep. But they are not ideal homes. The shelters are loud, and the animals stay in small cages. The people who work at shelters do their best to care for the animals, but the animals do not always get the attention or exercise they need.

To prevent so many animals from becoming homeless, pet owners should take good care of their pets. One of the best ways to care for pets is to spay or neuter them. This surgery prevents cats and dogs from having more babies. And that reduces the number of homeless animals that end up in shelters.

. . . .

1. **What is the passage mainly about?**

   Ⓐ the city of Salinas, California

   Ⓑ homeless animals in shelters

   Ⓒ how to attract visitors to animal shelters

   Ⓓ people who work at animal shelters

2. **Dogs in shelters probably do not get enough exercise because _____.**

   Ⓐ the workers do not enjoy walking them

   Ⓑ the workers think the dogs will be adopted soon

   Ⓒ there are too many animals for the workers to care for

   Ⓓ the workers are afraid of the dogs

3. **What is the result of spaying and neutering?**

   Ⓐ More puppies and kittens are adopted.

   Ⓑ Pets need less attention.

   Ⓒ Fewer animals become homeless.

   Ⓓ More people work at animal shelters.

4. **What can good homes offer that animal shelters cannot?**

   Ⓐ plenty of personal attention

   Ⓑ medical care

   Ⓒ a safe place to sleep

   Ⓓ food and water

Write It Right

Rewrite each sentence and correct the errors.

1. mr smith the art teacher lended me the book about picasso

_____

2. noises especially loud ones are frightening at night whispered fred

_____

3. my cat ollie naps wakes up and stretches and then she sleeps sum more

_____

4. kara hollered i hears you talking down there

_____

MATH TIME

Julie lives on a farm with sheep and geese. There are 10 animals, and they have a total of 32 legs. How many of each animal are there on the farm? Complete the function table to find the answer. Then circle the row with the correct answer.

Sheep (S)	Geese (G)	Total Number of Legs Rule: $(4 \times S) + (2 \times G)$
9	1	
8	2	
7	3	
6	4	

SPELL IT

> **Homophones** are words that sound alike but have different spellings and meanings.

Circle the correct spelling word for each meaning.

1. toward the front   forward   foreword

2. an admiring remark   compliment   complement

3. at last   finally   finely

4. not moving   stationary   stationery

5. helpers   assistance   assistants

6. people under a doctor's care   patients   patience

7. a short introduction to a book   forward   foreword

8. paper used to write letters   stationary   stationery

In My Own Words

If you had to decide between living without a television or living without junk food, which would you choose? Explain your choice.

LANGUAGE LINES

It is important to stay with the same **verb tense** from one sentence to the next. The tense should change only if the sentences are referring to different points in time.

Underline the verb in the first sentence. Fill in the blank in the second sentence with the correct tense of the word in parentheses.

1. Brad reports on school events. Mia _____ photographs for the paper.
   (take)

2. The story about the cafeteria was interesting. It _____ all the menus.
   (describe)

3. Brad named the "crumble burger" the worst dish. He _____ it "icky."
   (call)

4. The paper will run a story on the library next month. I _____ it.
   (write)

5. I am writing about fines for overdue books. Next year, the library _____ fines.
   (raise)

MATH TIME

A. Find **x** in each problem by adding or subtracting the same value on both sides of the equation.

$$x - 6 = 3$$
$$x - 6 + 6 = 3 + 6$$
$$x = 9$$

$$x + 2 = 7$$
$$x + 2 - 2 = 7 - 2$$
$$x = 5$$

1. $x + 4 = 5$ $x =$ _____

2. $x + 6 = 8$ $x =$ _____

3. $x - 5 = 12$ $x =$ _____

4. $x - 4 = 7$ $x =$ _____

B. Find **x** in each problem by multiplying or dividing the same value on both sides of the equation.

$$y \div 6 = 3$$
$$y \div 6 \times 6 = 3 \times 6$$
$$y = 18$$

$$2y = 8$$
$$2y \div 2 = 8 \div 2$$
$$y = 4$$

1. $6y = 24$ $y =$ _____

2. $3y = 18$ $y =$ _____

3. $y \div 1 = 7$ $y =$ _____

4. $y \div 8 = 6$ $y =$ _____

Read the story. Then answer the questions.

Mira's Visit

From the moment the airplane touched down at the Hong Kong airport, Mira knew she was in for an adventure. The busy airport was full of people bustling about. The people looked like they came from all over the world. Mira heard bits of conversation in many different languages.

Mira and her parents hurried to the hotel, where they checked in and dropped off their luggage. They were eager to begin exploring the city. Mira's dad brought a map and a detailed plan of what sights they would see.

The first stop on the list was the Hong Kong Wetland Park, just outside the city. The peaceful park had lots of places to walk, and Mira enjoyed sketching pictures of wildlife, including a crocodile lounging beside a private pool. On the train back to the city, the family marveled at the towering skyscrapers. Next, they stopped at the Science Museum, where Mira and her mom visited the World of Mirrors exhibit. After a lunch of local treats from a street-food cart, the family rushed to Victoria Harbor for the "Symphony of Lights." In the light show, beams of light were projected onto the buildings around the harbor and reflected off the calm waters below.

The family returned to the hotel, ready for a good night's sleep. Mira looked forward to another day of fun in Hong Kong. She was amazed to think of all they had done on their first day!

. . . .

1. **What did Mira and her family do before exploring Hong Kong?**

   Ⓐ They ate a meal at a street cart.

   Ⓑ They left their luggage at the hotel.

   Ⓒ They marveled at the city's skyscrapers.

   Ⓓ They rode on a train.

2. **What did the family plan to do first?**

   Ⓐ see a light show at the harbor

   Ⓑ go to a science museum

   Ⓒ go to a wildlife park

   Ⓓ enjoy lunch

3. **When did the family eat lunch?**

   Ⓐ after leaving the Science Museum

   Ⓑ before visiting the World of Mirrors exhibit

   Ⓒ after watching the "Symphony of Lights"

   Ⓓ after taking a nap at the hotel

4. **When did Mira first realize that Hong Kong was probably a busy city?**

   Ⓐ when she sketched a crocodile

   Ⓑ when she saw the towering skyscrapers

   Ⓒ when she and her family returned to the hotel

   Ⓓ when she and her family arrived at the airport

Vo·cab·u·lar·y

Roots are word parts that form the base of words and can give clues to a word's meaning.

viv = life   **nov = new**   **clin = lean**   **gen = birth**

A. Underline the root in each word in the box. Then write the word that matches each clue. Use a dictionary if necessary. The number under each word will be used in Activity B.

> gene   vivid   novice   survive   innovation
>
> novel   inclined   recliner   genealogy

1. someone who is a beginner: _____
   5

2. a record of your ancestors: _____
   7

3. a biological unit of heredity: _____
   3

4. new, different, or unusual: _____
   3

5. leaning in one direction: _____
   1

6. brightly colored: _____
   3

7. to continue to live: _____
   5

8. creative and new: _____
   6

9. a furniture piece that can be adjusted to lay back: _____
   4

B. Look at the number below each word in Activity A. Count that number of letters from the beginning of the word and circle the letter. Read the circled letters from top to bottom to reveal a word that means "sociable." Write the word below and circle its root.

_____

LANGUAGE LINES

The **antecedent** of a pronoun is the **noun** or nouns that the pronoun refers to or replaces.

The antecedent is underlined in each sentence or pair of sentences below. Write the correct pronoun on the line to match the antecedent.

1. <u>Students</u> are excited about the class business. _____ are making greeting cards.

2. <u>Amanda</u> got the idea for the cards. _____ has a card-making program at home.

3. The <u>business</u> should be simple to run. Here is how _____ will work.

4. Amanda will make some sample <u>cards</u>, and _____ will be shown to customers.

5. <u>Omar</u> will be in charge of taking orders for cards. _____ will collect all the orders.

6. Students working with <u>Trisha</u> will then make the cards. _____ is a good artist.

7. The cards will be delivered to the <u>customers</u>, at which time money will be

   collected from _____.

8. <u>I</u> would like to be a part of this class enterprise. It sounds exciting to _____.

In My Own Words

Who or what makes you laugh? Why?

Mind Jigglers

Abbreviations and Acronyms

Below are some common and uncommon abbreviations and acronyms used in text messaging. Use the numbers below to match each abbreviation at the bottom of the page with its meaning.

1. See you later!
2. high-five
3. Bye for now!
4. Excuse me.
5. are you
6. tomorrow
7. Oh, I see.
8. by the way
9. rolling on the floor laughing
10. I don't know.

11. anyone
12. nice to know
13. better known as
14. be back in a bit
15. two cents
16. no big deal
17. tons of time
18. Did you see that?
19. thinking of you
20. wonder

21. on the other hand
22. for crying out loud
23. in my humble opinion
24. away from keyboard
25. too good to be true
26. Don't hold your breath.
27. You've got to be kidding.
28. What did you say?

_____ .02   _____ BTW   _____ NE1   _____ TOY

_____ 2MORO   _____ CUL8ER   _____ NTK   _____ BBIAB

_____ 1DR   _____ DUST   _____ OIC   _____ XME

_____ 2G2BT   _____ DHYB   _____ OTOH   _____ WDYS

_____ 4COL   _____ ROFL   _____ BKA   _____ IMHO

_____ ^5   _____ IDK   _____ RU   _____ AFK

_____ BFN   _____ NBD   _____ TOT   _____ YG2BK

Connect the Dots

Plot the ordered pairs of numbers in the order in which they are listed in each set below, and connect them with straight lines. Start each new set of points with a new line. The lines will reveal a picture. The first line has been drawn for you in orange.

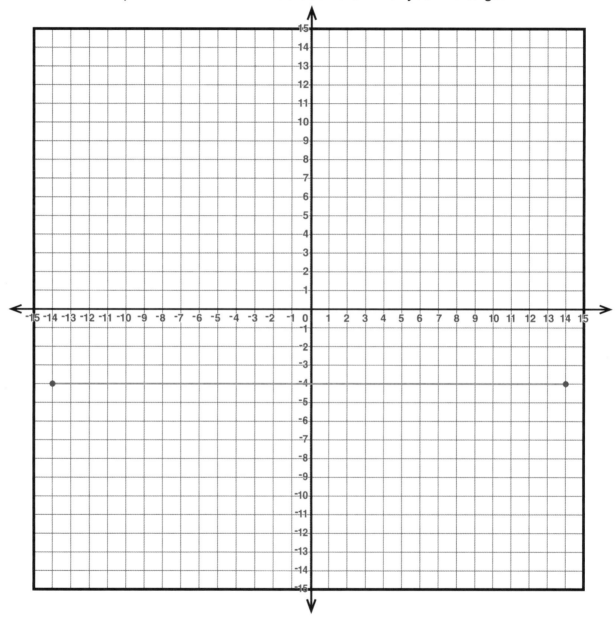

✔➤ Set 1: (−14, −4) (14, −4)

➤ Set 2: (−9, −2) (−8, −4) (−6, −4) (−5, −2)

➤ Set 3: (−8, −2) (−7, −3) (−6, −2)

➤ Set 4: (5, −2) (6, −4) (8, −4) (9, −2)

➤ Set 5: (6, −2) (7, −3) (8, −2)

➤ Set 6: (2, 4) (2, −2)

➤ Set 7: (7, 1) (5, 3) (3, 3) (3, 1) (7, 1)

➤ Set 8: (1, 1) (1, 3) (−2, 3) (−4, 1) (1, 1)

➤ Set 9: (11, −1) (13, −1) (13, −2) (−11, −2) (−11, 0) (−10, 1)
(−6, 1) (−2, 4) (5, 4) (9, 1) (11, 1) (11, −2)

Geography

Europe's Bodies of Water

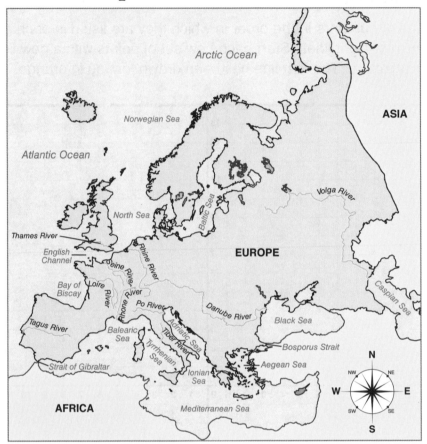

1. Which river flows into the Bay of Biscay? _____

2. Which river is located on an island? _____

3. Into which sea does the Volga River flow? _____

4. Which body of water connects the Black Sea
   to the Aegean Sea? _____

5. Which river is farthest west in Europe? _____

6. Which five seas are part of the Mediterranean Sea? List them.

   _____

   _____

WEEK 10

Check off each box as you complete the day's work.

Spelling Words

Antarctica

archaeology

cartographer

circumference

environment

hemisphere

international

parallelogram

patriotism

peninsula

perpendicular

rhombus

Get Creative!

Turn this line into a sailboat.

A Memorable Moment

What sticks in your mind about this week? Write about it.

_____

_____

_____

_____

_____

_____

_____

Reading Record

	Book Title	Pages	Time
Monday	_____	_____	_____
Tuesday	_____	_____	_____
Wednesday	_____	_____	_____
Thursday	_____	_____	_____
Friday	_____	_____	_____

Describe a character you read about this week.

_____

_____

_____

_____

_____

_____

Read the story. Then answer the questions.

The Amazing Phil

Sasha had simply wanted to get out of the car and stretch her legs. When she and her mom drove up to the ancient-looking gas station, neither of them was prepared to come face to face with a dinosaur. The sculpture loomed 20 feet over the car. It was a *T. rex*, and the green paint was peeling from its front legs, which dangled in the air. Sasha's mom wasn't sure what to make of the whole thing. "I wonder who created this," she said, shading her eyes from the bright sun.

"I did," said a shaky voice nearby. Sasha turned around to see an elderly man propped up on a cane. He steadied himself and pointed one finger up toward the *T. rex* sculpture. "He's the Amazing Phil," the man said. "I built him in 1955, right after I opened the gas station. He brought in a crowd for a long time, back when people didn't drive so fast." The man's weathered face broke into a soft smile.

"It's a great sculpture," Sasha's mom half-lied. "I like the colors. So, what's your name?"

"My name's Phil, too," said the man. He leaned back on his cane. "My wife is inside. She just made a pecan pie. Do you ladies like pie?"

Sasha looked at her mom. Her mom looked up at the dinosaur and then gazed up the road for a few awkward seconds. Then she smiled and looked at Phil. "Pecan pie is our favorite," she replied, closing the car door behind her.

· ·

1. **What is the author's main purpose for this story?**

   Ⓐ to suggest a fun place to go

   Ⓑ to encourage readers to be nice to older people

   Ⓒ to make fun of older people

   Ⓓ to tell a scary story about dinosaurs

2. **Which prediction could you correctly make based on the third paragraph?**

   Ⓐ Sasha and her mom will be kind to the man.

   Ⓑ Sasha's mom will buy the sculpture.

   Ⓒ The dinosaur will come to life.

   Ⓓ The car will accidentally hit the dinosaur.

3. **Why does the author include the detail that the dinosaur's paint is peeling?**

   Ⓐ to scare the reader

   Ⓑ to show that the dinosaur is old

   Ⓒ to suggest that the dinosaur is ugly

   Ⓓ to imply that the dinosaur was poorly made

4. **What will most likely happen next in the story?**

   Ⓐ Sasha will stretch her legs.

   Ⓑ Sasha and her mom will drive away.

   Ⓒ Sasha and her mom will eat pie.

   Ⓓ Sasha will wait in the car.

Write It Right

Rewrite each sentence and correct the errors.

1. the phone ringed just as mom was leafing the house

_____

2. my little couzen always says whats up

_____

3. i just finished reding a book called through my eyes by ruby bridges

_____

4. my littel sister wont stop bothering me to comes play out side

_____

MATH TIME

Factor trees can be used to find the prime factorization of any number. The following is an example of a factor tree for the prime factorization of the number 18:

Draw a factor tree to find the prime factorization of each of the following numbers:

16	20	24

SPELL IT

> Breaking a long word into **syllables**
> can help you remember the spelling.

Fill in the missing syllables to answer the clues with the spelling words for the week. If necessary, use a dictionary to help you.

1. someone who makes maps:

   car _____ ra _____

2. a square:

   _____ bus

3. an icy continent:

   Ant _____ ti _____

4. the study of ancient relics:

   ar _____ olo _____

5. a landform mostly surrounded by water:

   _____ nin _____ la

6. the outside of a circle:

   cir _____ fer _____

7. two or more countries:

   in _____ na _____ al

8. the natural world:

   _____ vi _____ ment

9. half of Earth:

   _____ _____ sphere

10. a rectangle:

    par _____ lel _____ gram

11. at a right angle:

    _____ pen _____ u _____

12. love of country:

    pa _____ _____ ism

In My Own Words

What is your favorite subject in school? Why do you like it?

LANGUAGE LINES

Many words in English come from other languages, such as Arabic, Spanish, and Hindi.

Use your understanding of word meanings to match each word with its language of origin. Write the letter of the origin next to the English word.

_____ 1. absurd

_____ 2. goulash

_____ 3. knapsack

_____ 4. ukulele

_____ 5. moccasin

_____ 6. bazaar

_____ 7. cookie

_____ 8. liberty

a. from the Hungarian *gulyás*

b. from a Hawaiian word for a type of instrument

c. from a Persian word meaning "market"

d. from the French word *liberté* meaning "freedom"

e. from an Algonquin word for *shoe*

f. from the Dutch word *knapzak*

g. from the French word *absurde*

h. from the Dutch word *koekje* meaning "little cake"

MATH TIME

Look at each set of fractions below and find the LCD (lowest common denominator).

1. $\frac{1}{5}, \frac{2}{3}$ LCD= _____

2. $\frac{4}{5}, \frac{2}{7}$ LCD= _____

3. $\frac{5}{6}, \frac{1}{3}$ LCD= _____

4. $\frac{3}{4}, \frac{9}{10}$ LCD= _____

5. $\frac{13}{15}, \frac{1}{20}$ LCD= _____

6. $\frac{19}{20}, \frac{1}{24}$ LCD= _____

7. $\frac{4}{9}, \frac{3}{5}$ LCD= _____

8. $\frac{7}{9}, \frac{5}{11}$ LCD= _____

Read the article. Then answer the questions.

Underground Mysteries

You may think that our knowledge of Earth is as solid as the ground beneath our feet. However, although scientists know some important facts about Earth's crust, many details are a mystery. To solve some of those mysteries, a group of Russian scientists drilled the deepest hole on the planet. Starting in the 1960s, researchers and special drillers began digging and drilling a hole in the northwestern part of Russia, on the Kola Peninsula. Before they were done, the Kola Superdeep Borehole was more than 7.5 miles deep.

Researchers unearthed many fascinating facts by drilling this hole. Miles below the surface, they found rock that was full of water, like a sponge. Scientists believed that the water had formed from extreme pressure inside the rock. The researchers also found a layer of tiny fossils about four miles down, deeper than anyone expected to find fossils. Another surprise was that Earth became much hotter—over 350°F—as drillers dug deeper.

Eventually, the drilling area became so hot that the drill bits melted. New holes would close as soon as they were dug. Realizing that better technology was needed, the team stopped drilling in 1994. The deepest hole ever drilled by humans was abandoned, but researchers at new sites have continued to investigate the mysteries within Earth's crust.

. . . .

1. **Why were scientists able to learn new things from the Kola Superdeep Borehole?**

   Ⓐ They had not tried drilling holes before.

   Ⓑ They devoted more money to the project.

   Ⓒ It was the deepest they had ever explored.

   Ⓓ Holes dug elsewhere did not reveal much.

2. **Why did the project most likely need the skills of special drillers?**

   Ⓐ The drilling project was unusual.

   Ⓑ The tiny fossils needed careful handling.

   Ⓒ Scientists knew little about Earth's crust.

   Ⓓ Special drillers stopped the holes from closing.

3. **What made the team realize they needed better technology to continue the work?**

   Ⓐ The tools damaged the fossils.

   Ⓑ The heat melted the drill bits.

   Ⓒ Workers were not interested in the project.

   Ⓓ Water deposits ruined the drill.

4. **The last sentence of the passage hints that _____.**

   Ⓐ Kola Superdeep Borehole was a waste of time

   Ⓑ superheated rock is found only in Russia

   Ⓒ other research sites were also abandoned

   Ⓓ discoveries are being made at other sites

Vo·cab·u·lar·y

An **idiom** is a phrase that means something different from what its individual words mean.

> **Idiom: Who let the cat out of the bag?**
> What it means: "Who told the secret?" or "Who ruined the surprise?"
> What it does *not* mean: "Who allowed a captured cat to escape?"

A. Rewrite each sentence by replacing the underlined words with the correct idiom from the box.

fork over	way off base	give me the lowdown
tightfisted	shooting the breeze	take the reins

1. Mr. Snively is <u>a person who doesn't like to spend money</u>.

   _____

2. Go ahead and <u>explain everything to me</u> about the surprise party.

   _____

3. No, you're <u>not even close to being right</u> about my age.

   _____

4. They were <u>chatting</u> when the alarm sounded.

   _____

5. We had to <u>pay</u> a lot of money just to get into the amusement park.

   _____

6. George will <u>assume control</u> on this project.

   _____

B. Write what a character on a TV crime drama might say to another character, using an idiom from Activity A.

_____

_____

LANGUAGE LINES

Adjectives modify or describe nouns or pronouns.
A **predicate adjective** follows a linking verb in a sentence.

> **The comedian was hilarious.**
> linking verb ⬏   ⬑ predicate adjective

Underline each adjective in the sentences below. Write the letters *PA* above each predicate adjective. The first one has been done for you.

1. The telescopes that tell scientists about <u>faraway</u> stars are <u>powerful</u>. **PA**

2. The precise information that the giant instruments transmit to the scientists is important.

3. Most of the data from the telescopes is useful, although some is unnecessary.

4. Throughout history, people have found stars to be mysterious and fascinating.

5. Even with plentiful information, people are awestruck by a starry sky.

6. Imagine living long ago and seeing an unexplained sight that was amazing.

In My Own Words

If you could go anywhere in the world, where would it be? What would you do there?

Mind Jigglers

At the Movies

Five friends went to see five different movies. Each child got a different snack to eat during the movie. Read the clues to find out which movie each child watched and what snack each child purchased. Make an **X** in a square when it cannot be an answer. Draw a circle when it is a correct answer.

		Movies					Snacks				
		Shrek 27	Harry Potato	Finding Nemo Again	Bambi Goes to College	Rats in Restaurants	Popcorn	Red Vines	M&M's	Junior Mints	Ice-Cream Bar
Children	Michael										
	Pam										
	Dwight										
	Angela										
	Jim										

1. Neither of the girls bought candy for a snack.

2. Neither Michael nor Angela saw a movie about animals.

3. Jim gave some of his Red Vines to the girl who saw *Rats in Restaurants*.

4. Angela told the person who saw *Harry Potato* that she doesn't like popcorn.

5. Dwight does *not* like candy that comes in different colors.

6. The person who had Junior Mints would not share any with the person who saw *Finding Nemo Again*.

MATH TIME

What's Your GCF?

Find the Greatest Common Factor (GCF) for each of the following sets of numbers:

> ### Remember:
> The **Greatest Common Factor (GCF)** is the highest number that divides exactly into two or more numbers.
>
> The GCF of **12** and **24** is **12**.
> The GCF of **4, 10,** and **16** is **2.**

1. 2, 4   GCF=_____

2. 3, 9   GCF=_____

3. 9, 12   GCF=_____

4. 4, 12   GCF=_____

5. 12, 15   GCF=_____

6. 6, 8   GCF=_____

7. 4, 8, 10   GCF=_____

8. 5, 10, 25   GCF=_____

9. 6, 10, 18   GCF=_____

10. 12, 24, 48   GCF=_____

11. 15, 20, 105   GCF=_____

12. 11, 33, 44   GCF=_____

Geography

The Countries of Eastern Africa

1. How many countries are in Eastern Africa? _____

2. What is the largest island country in Eastern Africa? _____

3. Which country is completely surrounded by other Eastern African countries? _____

4. What is the northernmost country in Eastern Africa? _____

5. Which two countries are archipelagos?

_____

6. Which two small countries help form the northwest border of Tanzania?

_____

Answer Key

Checking your child's work is an important part of learning. It allows you to see what your child knows well and what areas need more practice. It also provides an opportunity for you to help your child understand that making mistakes is a part of learning.

The answer key pages can be used in several ways:

➤ Remove the answer pages and give the book to your child. Go over the answers with him or her as each day's work is completed.

➤ Leave the answer pages in the book and give the practice pages to your child one day at a time.

➤ Leave the answer pages in the book so your child can check his or her own work as the pages are completed. It is still important to review the pages with your child if you use this method.

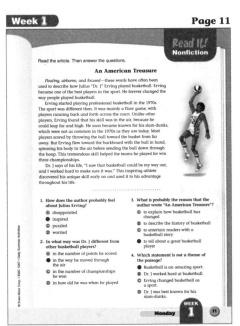

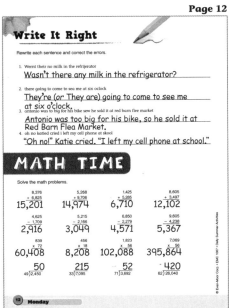

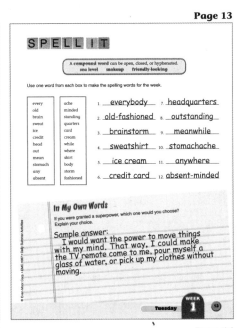

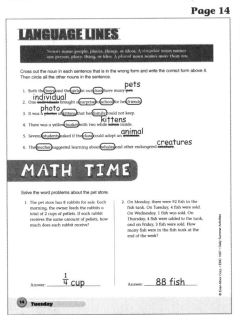

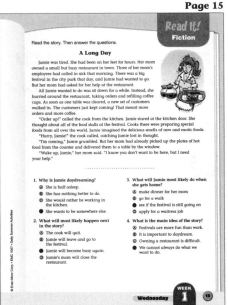

Page 17

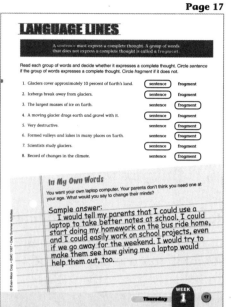

LANGUAGE LINES

A sentence must express a complete thought. A group of words that does not express a complete thought is called a fragment.

Read each group of words and decide whether it expresses a complete thought. Circle *sentence* if the group of words expresses a complete thought. Circle *fragment* if it does not.

1. Glaciers cover approximately 10 percent of Earth's land. **(sentence)** fragment
2. Icebergs break away from glaciers. **(sentence)** fragment
3. The largest masses of ice on Earth. sentence **(fragment)**
4. A moving glacier drags earth and gravel with it. **(sentence)** fragment
5. Very destructive. sentence **(fragment)**
6. Formed valleys and lakes in many places on Earth. sentence **(fragment)**
7. Scientists study glaciers. **(sentence)** fragment
8. Record of changes in the climate. sentence **(fragment)**

In My Own Words

You want your own laptop computer. Your parents don't think you need one at your age. What would you say to change their minds?

Sample answer:
I would tell my parents that I could use a laptop to take better notes at school. I could start doing my homework on the bus ride home, and I could easily work on school projects, even if we go away for the weekend. I would try to make them see how giving me a laptop would help them out, too.

Thursday WEEK 1 17

Page 18

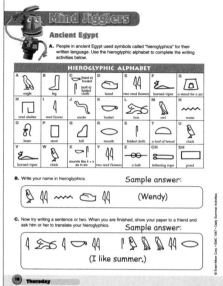

Mind Jigglers

Ancient Egypt

A. People in ancient Egypt used symbols called "hieroglyphics" for their written language. Use the hieroglyphic alphabet to complete the writing activities below.

HIEROGLYPHIC ALPHABET

B. Write your name in hieroglyphics. Sample answer:

(Wendy)

C. Now try writing a sentence or two. When you are finished, show your paper to a friend and ask him or her to translate your hieroglyphics. Sample answer:

(I like summer.)

18 Thursday

Page 19

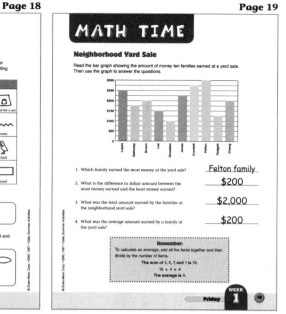

MATH TIME

Neighborhood Yard Sale

Read the bar graph showing the amount of money ten families earned at a yard sale. Then use the graph to answer the questions.

1. Which family earned the most money at the yard sale? Felton family
2. What is the difference in dollar amount between the most money earned and the least money earned? $200
3. What was the total amount earned by the families at the neighborhood yard sale? $2,000
4. What was the average amount earned by a family at the yard sale? $200

Remember:
To calculate an average, add all the items together and then divide by the number of items.
The sum of 3, 5, 7, and 1 is 16.
16 ÷ 4 = 4
The average is 4.

Friday WEEK 1 19

Page 20

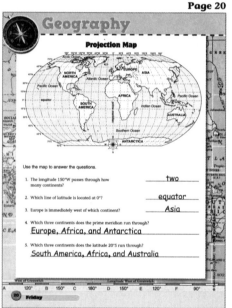

Geography

Projection Map

Use the map to answer the questions.

1. The longitude 150°W passes through how many continents? two
2. Which line of latitude is located at 0°? equator
3. Europe is immediately west of which continent? Asia
4. Which three continents does the prime meridian run through? Europe, Africa, and Antarctica
5. Which three continents does the latitude 20°S run through? South America, Africa, and Australia

20 Friday

Week 2

Page 23

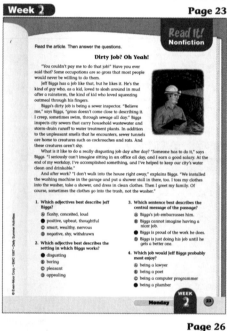

Read It! Nonfiction

Read the article. Then answer the questions.

Dirty Job? Oh Yeah!

"You couldn't pay me to do that job!" Have you ever said that? Some occupations are so gross that most people would never be willing to do them.

Jeff Biggs has a job like that, but he likes it. He's the kind of guy who, as a kid, loved to slosh around in mud after a rainstorm, the kind of kid who loved squeezing oatmeal through his fingers.

Biggs's dirty job is being a sewer inspector. "Believe me," says Biggs, "gross doesn't come close to describing it. I creep, sometimes swim, through sewage all day." Biggs inspects city sewers that carry household wastewater and storm-drain runoff to water treatment plants. In addition to the unpleasant smells that he encounters, sewer tunnels are home to creatures such as cockroaches and rats. And these creatures aren't shy.

What is it like to do a really disgusting job day after day? "Someone has to do it," says Biggs. "I seriously can't imagine sitting in an office all day, and I earn a good salary. At the end of my workday, I've accomplished something, and I've helped to keep our city's water clean and drinkable."

And after work? "I don't walk into the house right away," explains Biggs. "We installed the washing machine in the garage and put a shower stall in there, too. I toss my clothes into the washer, take a shower, and dress in clean clothes. Then I greet my family. Of course, sometimes the clothes go into the trash, not the washer."

1. **Which adjectives best describe Jeff Biggs?**
   - Ⓐ flashy, conceited, loud
   - ● positive, upbeat, thoughtful
   - Ⓒ smart, wealthy, nervous
   - Ⓓ negative, shy, withdrawn
2. **Which adjective best describes the setting in which Biggs works?**
   - ● disgusting
   - Ⓑ boring
   - Ⓒ pleasant
   - Ⓓ appealing
3. **Which sentence best describes the central message of the passage?**
   - Ⓐ Biggs's job embarrasses him.
   - Ⓑ Biggs cannot imagine having a nicer job.
   - ● Biggs is proud of the work he does.
   - Ⓓ Biggs is just doing his job until he gets a better one.
4. **Which job would Jeff Biggs probably most enjoy?**
   - Ⓐ being a lawyer
   - Ⓑ being a poet
   - Ⓒ being a computer programmer
   - ● being a plumber

Monday WEEK 2 23

Page 24

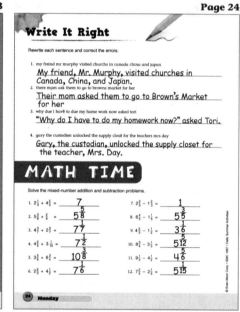

Write It Right

Rewrite each sentence and correct the errors.

1. my freind mr murphy visited churchs in canada china and japan
   My friend, Mr. Murphy, visited churches in Canada, China, and Japan.
2. there mom ask them to go to browns market for her
   Their mom asked them to go to Brown's Market for her
3. why due i have to due my home work now asked tori
   "Why do I have to do my homework now?" asked Tori.
4. gary the custodien unlocked the supply closit for the teachers mrs day
   Gary, the custodian, unlocked the supply closet for the teacher, Mrs. Day.

MATH TIME

Solve the mixed-number addition and subtraction problems.

1. $2\frac{1}{3} + 4\frac{2}{3} =$ 7
2. $5\frac{3}{8} + \frac{2}{8} =$ $5\frac{5}{8}$
3. $4\frac{3}{7} + 2\frac{5}{7} =$ $7\frac{1}{7}$
4. $4\frac{2}{5} + 3\frac{1}{10} =$ $7\frac{1}{2}$
5. $3\frac{5}{8} + 6\frac{3}{4} =$ $10\frac{3}{8}$
6. $2\frac{2}{3} + 4\frac{1}{2} =$ $7\frac{1}{6}$
7. $2\frac{2}{3} - 1\frac{2}{3} =$ 1
8. $6\frac{4}{5} - 1\frac{1}{5} =$ $5\frac{3}{5}$
9. $4\frac{2}{3} - 1\frac{1}{2} =$ $3\frac{1}{6}$
10. $8\frac{3}{4} - 3\frac{1}{3} =$ $5\frac{5}{12}$
11. $9\frac{1}{3} - 4\frac{1}{2} =$ $4\frac{5}{6}$
12. $7\frac{2}{5} - 2\frac{1}{3} =$ $5\frac{1}{15}$

24 Monday

Page 25

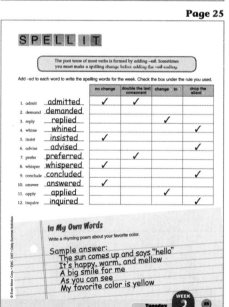

SPELL IT

The past tense of most verbs is formed by adding *–ed*. Sometimes you must make a spelling change before adding the *–ed* ending.

Add *–ed* to each word to write the spelling words for the week. Check the box under the rule you used.

		no change	double the last consonant	change y to i	drop the silent e
1. admit	admitted	✓	✓		
2. demand	demanded				
3. reply	replied			✓	
4. whine	whined				✓
5. insist	insisted	✓			
6. advise	advised				✓
7. prefer	preferred		✓		
8. whisper	whispered	✓			
9. conclude	concluded				✓
10. answer	answered	✓			
11. apply	applied			✓	
12. inquire	inquired				✓

In My Own Words

Write a rhyming poem about your favorite color.

Sample answer:
The sun comes up and says "hello"
It's happy, warm, and mellow
A big smile for me
As you can see
My favorite color is yellow

Tuesday WEEK 2 25

Page 26

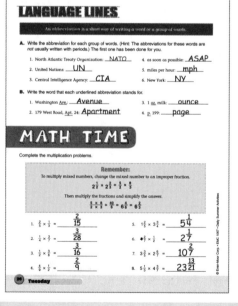

LANGUAGE LINES

An abbreviation is a short way of writing a word or a group of words.

A. Write the abbreviation for each group of words. (Hint: The abbreviations for these words are *not* usually written with periods.) The first one has been done for you.

1. North Atlantic Treaty Organization: NATO
2. United Nations: UN
3. Central Intelligence Agency: CIA
4. as soon as possible: ASAP
5. miles per hour: mph
6. New York: NY

B. Write the word that each underlined abbreviation stands for.

1. Washington <u>Ave.</u>: Avenue
2. 179 West Road, <u>Apt.</u> 24: Apartment
3. 1 <u>oz.</u> milk: ounce
4. <u>p.</u> 199: page

MATH TIME

Complete the multiplication problems.

Remember:
To multiply mixed numbers, change the mixed number to an improper fraction.
$$2\frac{1}{2} \times 2\frac{2}{3} = \frac{5}{2} \times \frac{8}{3}$$
Then multiply the fractions and simplify the answer.
$$\frac{5 \times 8}{2 \times 3} = \frac{40}{6} = 6\frac{4}{6} = 6\frac{2}{3}$$

1. $\frac{2}{5} \times \frac{1}{3} =$ $\frac{2}{15}$
2. $\frac{1}{4} \times \frac{3}{7} =$ $\frac{3}{28}$
3. $\frac{1}{2} \times \frac{3}{8} =$ $\frac{3}{16}$
4. $\frac{4}{9} \times \frac{1}{2} =$ $\frac{2}{9}$
5. $1\frac{2}{5} \times 3\frac{3}{4} =$ $5\frac{1}{4}$
6. [illegible]$\frac{2}{7} \times \frac{1}{2} =$ $2\frac{1}{7}$
7. $3\frac{3}{5} \times 2\frac{6}{7} =$ $10\frac{2}{7}$
8. $5\frac{1}{3} \times 4\frac{3}{7} =$ $23\frac{13}{21}$

26 Tuesday

Page 27

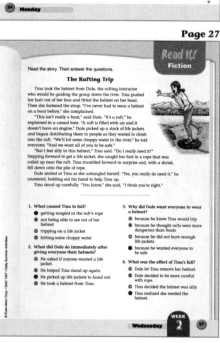

Read It! Fiction

Read the story. Then answer the questions.

The Rafting Trip

Tina took the helmet from Dale, the rafting instructor who would be guiding the group down the river. Tina pushed her hair out of her face and fitted the helmet on her head. Then she fastened the strap. "I've never had to wear a helmet on a boat before," she complained.

"This isn't really a boat," said Dale. "It's a raft," he explained in a casual tone. "A raft is filled with air and it doesn't have an engine." Dale picked up a stack of life jackets and began distributing them to people as they waited to climb into the raft. "We'll hit some choppy water in the river," he told everyone. "And we want all of you to be safe."

"But I feel silly in this helmet," Tina said. "Do I really need it?" Stepping forward to get a life jacket, she caught her foot in a rope that was coiled up near the raft. Tina stumbled forward in surprise and, with a shriek, fell down onto the pile of rope.

Dale smiled at Tina as she untangled herself. "Yes, you really do need it," he answered, holding out his hand to help Tina up.

Tina stood up carefully. "You know," she said, "I think you're right."

1. **What caused Tina to fall?**
   - ● getting tangled in the raft's rope
   - Ⓑ not being able to see out of her helmet
   - Ⓒ tripping on a life jacket
   - Ⓓ hitting some choppy water
2. **What did Dale do immediately after giving everyone their helmets?**
   - Ⓐ He asked if anyone wanted a life jacket.
   - Ⓑ He helped Tina stand up again.
   - ● He picked up life jackets to hand out.
   - Ⓓ He took a helmet from Tina.
3. **Why did Dale want everyone to wear a helmet?**
   - Ⓐ because he knew Tina would trip
   - Ⓑ because he thought rafts were more dangerous than boats
   - Ⓒ because he did not have enough life jackets
   - ● because he wanted everyone to be safe
4. **What was the effect of Tina's fall?**
   - Ⓐ Dale let Tina remove her helmet.
   - Ⓑ Dale decided to be more careful with rope.
   - Ⓒ Tina decided the helmet was silly.
   - ● Tina realized she needed the helmet.

Wednesday WEEK 2 27

Page 28

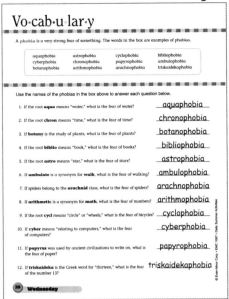

Vo·cab·u·lar·y

A **phobia** is a very strong fear of something. The words in the box are examples of phobias.

aquaphobia	astrophobia	cyclophobia	bibliophobia
cyberphobia	chronophobia	papyrophobia	ambulophobia
botanophobia	arithmophobia	arachnophobia	triskaidekaphobia

Use the names of the phobias in the box above to answer each question below.

1. If the root **aqua** means "water," what is the fear of water? aquaphobia
2. If the root **chron** means "time," what is the fear of time? chronophobia
3. If **botany** is the study of plants, what is the fear of plants? botanophobia
4. If the root **biblio** means "book," what is the fear of books? bibliophobia
5. If the root **astro** means "star," what is the fear of stars? astrophobia
6. If **ambulate** is a synonym for **walk**, what is the fear of walking? ambulophobia
7. If spiders belong to the **arachnid** class, what is the fear of spiders? arachnophobia
8. If **arithmetic** is a synonym for **math**, what is the fear of numbers? arithmophobia
9. If the root **cycl** means "circle" or "wheels," what is the fear of bicycles? cyclophobia
10. If **cyber** means "relating to computers," what is the fear of computers? cyberphobia
11. If **papyrus** was used by ancient civilizations to write on, what is the fear of paper? papyrophobia
12. If **triskaideka** is the Greek word for "thirteen," what is the fear of the number 13? triskaidekaphobia

28 Wednesday

Page 29

LANGUAGE LINES

The topic sentence introduces the main idea of a paragraph.

Read the paragraph and underline the topic sentence. Then summarize the main idea and list three supporting details below it.

Seeds spread themselves around in many different ways. Some seeds move on the wind. They have winglike parts to catch the wind. Other seeds have hooks or stickers. They latch onto the fur of animals and are carried away as the animals roam. Some seeds disperse themselves by floating on water. We humans move seeds, too, when we plant them in our yards and gardens.

Main Idea: Sample answers:
Seeds travel in different ways.

Details:

1. Seeds move on the wind.
2. Seeds latch onto the fur of animals.
3. People move seeds.

In My Own Words

What do you think is the most important human invention ever created? Explain your choice.

Sample answer:
I think the most important human invention is the airplane. Being able to fly means that we can go anywhere on the planet in a reasonable amount of time. Airplanes have allowed people to reach and experience faraway lands that would take too long to get to on foot, in a car, or by boat. Planes have brought people together from all over the world.

Thursday WEEK 2 29

Page 30

Mind Jigglers

In My Room

A. Write four adjectives to describe your room. Sample answers:

1. fun
2. rectangular
3. cluttered
4. messy

What is... Sample answers:

the oldest thing in your room? my bed

the newest thing in your room? a new pair of jeans

the thing in your room you most treasure? my TV

something in your room you have outgrown? my first teddy bear

B. Use the clues to name things you would probably find in a bedroom. Then find the words in the word search. Words may appear across, down, or diagonally.

- where you dream: bed
- where clothes hang: closet
- taped to a wall: poster
- a homework surface: desk
- a head cushion: pillow
- gives you a view: window
- a place for books: shelf
- has a bulb: lamp
- has a seat: chair

R	B	A	D	R	C	B
M	L	E	I	B	L	P
T	P	A	D	A	O	S
X	H	O	G	S	S	H
C	D	E	S	M	E	E
P	H	E	A	T	T	L
I	R	P	S	O	E	F
L	O	Z	P	K	E	R
L	W	I	N	D	O	W
O	L	E	H	C	A	R
W	L	A	M	P	I	J

30 Thursday

Page 31

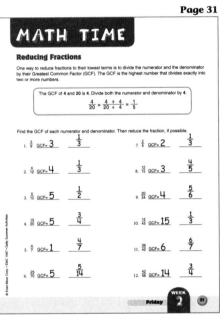

MATH TIME

Reducing Fractions

One way to reduce fractions to their lowest terms is to divide the numerator and the denominator by their Greatest Common Factor (GCF). The GCF is the highest number that divides exactly into two or more numbers.

The GCF of **4** and **20** is **4**. Divide both the numerator and denominator by **4**.

$$\frac{4}{20} = \frac{4 \div 4}{20 \div 4} = \frac{1}{5}$$

Find the GCF of each numerator and denominator. Then reduce the fraction, if possible.

1. $\frac{3}{9}$ GCF= 3 $\frac{1}{3}$
2. $\frac{4}{12}$ GCF= 4 $\frac{1}{3}$
3. $\frac{5}{10}$ GCF= 5 $\frac{1}{2}$
4. $\frac{15}{20}$ GCF= 5 $\frac{3}{4}$
5. $\frac{4}{7}$ GCF= 1 $\frac{4}{7}$
6. $\frac{25}{70}$ GCF= 5 $\frac{5}{14}$
7. $\frac{2}{6}$ GCF= 2 $\frac{1}{3}$
8. $\frac{12}{15}$ GCF= 3 $\frac{4}{5}$
9. $\frac{20}{24}$ GCF= 4 $\frac{5}{6}$
10. $\frac{15}{45}$ GCF= 15 $\frac{1}{3}$
11. $\frac{36}{42}$ GCF= 6 $\frac{6}{7}$
12. $\frac{42}{56}$ GCF= 14 $\frac{3}{4}$

Friday WEEK 2 31

Page 32

Geography

Antarctica

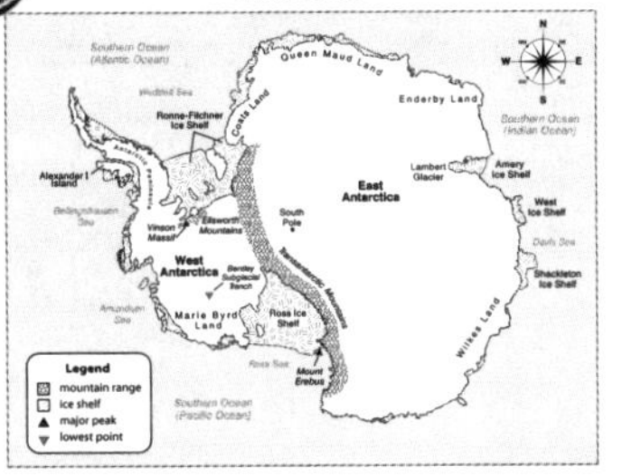

1. Which mountain range runs through the middle of the continent? Transantarctic
2. What is the name of the major peak just south of the Ronne-Filchner Ice Shelf? Vinson Massif
3. What is the name of the mountain peak bordering the Ross Ice Shelf? Mount Erebus
4. Which ice shelf is closest to the Lambert Glacier? Amery Ice Shelf
5. What is the name of the peninsula in West Antarctica? Antarctic Peninsula
6. What is the name of the lowest point in Antarctica? Bentley Subglacial Trench

32 Friday

Week 3 — Page 35

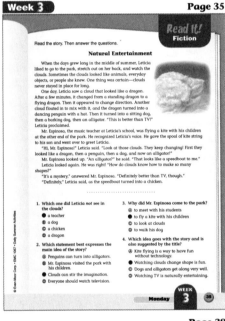

Read It! Fiction

Read the story. Then answer the questions.

Natural Entertainment

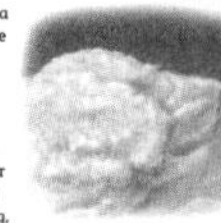

When the days grew long in the middle of summer, Leticia liked to go to the park, stretch out on her back, and watch the clouds. Sometimes the clouds looked like animals, everyday objects, or people she knew. One thing was certain—clouds never stayed in place for long.

One day, Leticia saw a cloud that looked like a dragon. After a few minutes, it changed from a standing dragon to a flying dragon. Then it appeared to change direction. Another cloud floated in to mix with it, and the dragon turned into a dancing penguin with a hat. Then it turned into a sitting dog, then a barking dog, then an alligator. "This is better than TV!" Leticia proclaimed.

Mr. Espinosa, the music teacher at Leticia's school, was flying a kite with his children at the other end of the park. He recognized Leticia's voice. He gave the spool of kite string to his son and went over to greet Leticia.

"Hi, Mr. Espinosa!" Leticia said. "Look at those clouds. They keep changing! First they looked like a dragon, then a penguin, then a dog, and now an alligator!"

Mr. Espinosa looked up. "An alligator?" he said. "That looks like a speedboat to me."

Leticia looked again. He was right! "How do clouds know how to make so many shapes?"

"It's a mystery," answered Mr. Espinosa. "Definitely better than TV, though."

"Definitely," Leticia said, as the speedboat turned into a chicken.

1. **Which one did Leticia *not* see in the clouds?**
   - ● a teacher
   - Ⓑ a dog
   - Ⓒ a chicken
   - Ⓓ a dragon
2. **Which statement best expresses the main idea of the story?**
   - Ⓐ Penguins can turn into alligators.
   - Ⓑ Mr. Espinosa visited the park with his children.
   - ● Clouds can stir the imagination.
   - Ⓓ Everyone should watch television.
3. **Why did Mr. Espinosa come to the park?**
   - Ⓐ to meet with his students
   - ● to fly a kite with his children
   - Ⓒ to look at clouds
   - Ⓓ to walk his dog
4. **Which idea goes with the story and is also suggested by the title?**
   - Ⓐ Kite flying is a way to have fun without technology.
   - ● Watching clouds change shape is fun.
   - Ⓒ Dogs and alligators get along very well.
   - Ⓓ Watching TV is naturally entertaining.

Monday WEEK 3 35

Page 36

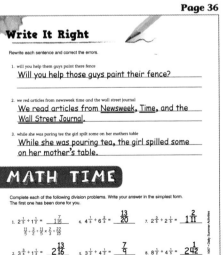

Write It Right

Rewrite each sentence and correct the errors.

1. will you help them guys paint there fence
   Will you help those guys paint their fence?
2. we red articles from newsweek time and the wall street journal
   We read articles from Newsweek, Time, and the Wall Street Journal.
3. while she was poring tee the girl spilt some on her mothers table
   While she was pouring tea, the girl spilled some on her mother's table.

MATH TIME

Complete each of the following division problems. Write your answer in the simplest form. The first one has been done for you.

1. $2\frac{1}{5} \div 1\frac{1}{2} = 1\frac{7}{15}$
   $\frac{11}{5} \div \frac{3}{2} = \frac{11}{5} \times \frac{2}{3} = \frac{22}{15}$
2. $3\frac{3}{4} \div 1\frac{1}{3} = 2\frac{13}{16}$
3. $2\frac{1}{2} \div 1\frac{1}{4} = 2$
4. $4\frac{1}{3} \div 6\frac{2}{3} = \frac{13}{20}$
5. $3\frac{1}{2} \div 4\frac{1}{2} = \frac{7}{9}$
6. $7\frac{1}{2} \div 8 = \frac{15}{16}$
7. $2\frac{3}{5} \div 2\frac{1}{5} = 1\frac{2}{11}$
8. $8\frac{1}{2} \div 4\frac{1}{5} = 2\frac{1}{42}$
9. $9\frac{4}{5} \div 6\frac{2}{5} = 1\frac{17}{32}$

36 Monday

Page 37

SPELL IT

A **suffix** is a word part added to the end of a word that changes its meaning.

Add the suffix *–ment, –ful,* or *–less* to each base word to make the spelling word for the week. Then circle the base word that could be joined with another suffix to make a new word. Write the new word next to the spelling word.

1. govern ment
2. tire less
3. (thought) ful thoughtless
4. amaze ment
5. humor less
6. (cheer) ful cheerless
7. effort less
8. judg ment
9. grate ful
10. (care) ful careless
11. (power) less powerful
12. enjoy ment

In My Own Words

If you found a magic cell phone that allowed you to talk to anyone—alive, dead, real, or fictional—whom would you call and why? What would you say?

Sample answer:
I would call President Barack Obama and ask him what secrets he learned about the world when he became president. For example, is there, in fact, a place in Nevada called Area 51, where the government stores UFOs and other alien artifacts? Does the government know whether there is life on other planets? I would be very curious to know whether these questions have answers and if the president was told about them when he took power.

Tuesday WEEK 3 37

Page 38

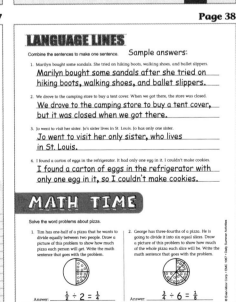

LANGUAGE LINES

Combine the sentences to make one sentence. Sample answers:

1. Marilyn bought some sandals. She tried on hiking boots, walking shoes, and ballet slippers.
   Marilyn bought some sandals after she tried on hiking boots, walking shoes, and ballet slippers.
2. We drove to the camping store to buy a tent cover. When we got there, the store was closed.
   We drove to the camping store to buy a tent cover, but it was closed when we got there.
3. Jo went to visit her sister. Jo's sister lives in St. Louis. Jo has only one sister.
   Jo went to visit her only sister, who lives in St. Louis.
4. I found a carton of eggs in the refrigerator. It had only one egg in it. I couldn't make cookies.
   I found a carton of eggs in the refrigerator with only one egg in it, so I couldn't make cookies.

MATH TIME

Solve the word problems about pizza.

1. Tim has one-half of a pizza that he wants to divide equally between two people. Draw a picture of this problem to show how much pizza each person will get. Write the math sentence that goes with the problem.

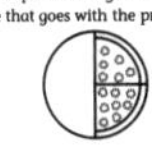

Answer: $\frac{1}{2} \div 2 = \frac{1}{4}$

2. George has three-fourths of a pizza. He is going to divide it into six equal slices. Draw a picture of this problem to show how much of the whole pizza each slice will be. Write the math sentence that goes with the problem.

Answer: $\frac{3}{4} \div 6 = \frac{1}{8}$

38 Tuesday

Answer Key 131

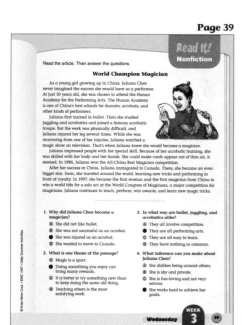

Page 39

Read It! Nonfiction

Read the article. Then answer the questions.

World Champion Magician

As a young girl growing up in China, Juliana Chen never imagined the success she would have as a performer. At just 10 years old, she was chosen to attend the Hunan Academy for the Performing Arts. The Hunan Academy is one of China's best schools for dancers, acrobats, and other kinds of performers.

Juliana first trained in ballet. Then she studied juggling and acrobatics and joined a famous acrobatic troupe. But the work was physically difficult, and Juliana injured her leg several times. While she was recovering from one of her injuries, Juliana watched a magic show on television. That's when Juliana knew she would become a magician.

Juliana impressed people with her special skill. Because of her acrobatic training, she was skilled with her body and her hands. She could make cards appear out of thin air, it seemed. In 1986, Juliana won the All-China Best Magician competition.

After her success in China, Juliana immigrated to Canada. There, she became an even bigger star. Soon, she traveled around the world, learning new tricks and performing in front of royalty. In 1997, she became the first woman and the first magician from China to win a world title for a solo act at the World Congress of Magicians, a major competition for magicians. Juliana continues to teach, perform, win awards, and learn new magic tricks.

1. Why did Juliana Chen become a magician?
- Ⓐ She did not like ballet.
- Ⓑ She was not successful as an acrobat.
- ● She was injured as an acrobat.
- Ⓓ She wanted to move to Canada.

2. What is one theme of the passage?
- Ⓐ Magic is a sport.
- ● Doing something you enjoy can bring many rewards.
- Ⓒ It is better to try something new than to keep doing the same old thing.
- Ⓓ Teaching others is the most satisfying work.

3. In what way are ballet, juggling, and acrobatics alike?
- Ⓐ They all involve competition.
- ● They are all performing arts.
- Ⓒ They are all easy to learn.
- Ⓓ They have nothing in common.

4. What inference can you make about Juliana Chen?
- Ⓐ She dislikes being around others.
- Ⓑ She is shy and private.
- Ⓒ She is fun-loving and not very serious.
- ● She works hard to achieve her goals.

Wednesday WEEK 3 39

Page 40

Vo·cab·u·lar·y

Synonyms are words that have the same or nearly the same meaning.
Funny and **humorous** are *synonyms*.

Heteronyms are words that are spelled the same but have different meanings and pronunciations.
Desert (a dry region) and **desert** (to withdraw from or abandon) are *heteronyms*.

A. Simon has something interesting to tell you. To find out what it is, do what Simon says—and *only* what Simon says.

1. Simon says, "Cross off all synonyms for **eat** in column C and in row three."
2. Simon says, "Cross off all country names."
3. Simon says, "Cross off all words in column D and in row 5 that could be heteronyms."
4. Cross off all words that contain a vowel.
5. Simon says, "Cross off all words in column A that refer to people."
6. Simon says, "Cross off all compound words in row six and in column E."
7. Simon says, "Cross off all words with fewer than three letters."

	A	B	C	D	E	F
1	~~Canada~~	~~it~~	~~consume~~	American	~~overeat~~	~~we~~
2	~~artists~~	colonists	~~it~~	~~object~~	~~Germany~~	ate
3	popcorn	~~nibble~~	~~feast~~	~~conduct~~	like	~~gobble~~
4	~~doctors~~	~~Japan~~	cereal	~~separate~~	~~watermelon~~	with
5	~~students~~	~~as~~	~~dine~~	milk	~~desert~~	and
6	~~milkshake~~	sugar	~~munch~~	~~cupcake~~	~~mealtime~~	~~Mexico~~

B. Write out the remaining ten words to discover a fascinating fact.

American colonists ate popcorn like cereal with milk and sugar.

40 Wednesday

Page 41

LANGUAGE LINES

The complete subject of a sentence includes the main noun or pronoun and related words. The complete predicate contains the verb and related words.

Underline the complete subject, and circle the complete predicate. The first one has been done for you.

1. My world studies class | is planning an international dinner.
2. Our teacher | will make an exotic dish.
3. Mr. Crosby | has offered to bring chicken curry with rice.
4. Curry | is a mixture of spices popular in India.
5. My friend Rachel | is bringing a Hungarian dish with noodles.
6. My mother | might help me make fried okra.
7. Fried okra | is a popular vegetable dish in the southern United States.
8. All of the seventh and eighth graders | are invited to the dinner.
9. Our principal, Ms. Rodriguez, | can't be there.
10. Ms. Rodriguez and her husband | are going on a trip to Spain.

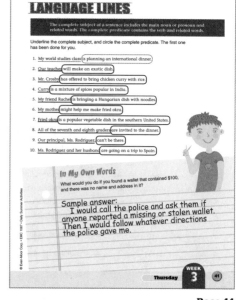

In My Own Words

What would you do if you found a wallet that contained $100, and there was no name and address in it?

Sample answer:
I would call the police and ask them if anyone reported a missing or stolen wallet. Then I would follow whatever directions the police gave me.

Thursday WEEK 3 41

Page 42

Mind Jogglers

Friends

Use the names in the box to match each character below with his or her friend.

Abu	Jill	Ron	Sam	Toto	Jane	Dale
Ernie	Luigi	Clark	Juliet	Piglet	Robin	Barbie
Timon	Louise	Wendy	Scooby	Wilbur	Minnie	Tweety
Barney	Watson	Patrick	Donkey	Milhouse	Woodstock	Daffy Duck

1. Batman & Robin
2. Chip & Dale
3. Thelma & Louise
4. Sherlock & Watson
5. Harry & Ron
6. Charlotte & Wilbur
7. Bugs Bunny & Daffy Duck
8. SpongeBob & Patrick
9. Bert & Ernie
10. Jack & Jill
11. Shrek & Donkey
12. Lewis & Clark
13. Mario & Luigi
14. Frodo & Sam
15. Pooh & Piglet
16. Shaggy & Scooby
17. Romeo & Juliet
18. Pumbaa & Timon
19. Tarzan & Jane
20. Peter Pan & Wendy
21. Fred & Barney
22. Mickey & Minnie
23. Dorothy & Toto
24. Snoopy & Woodstock
25. Bart & Milhouse
26. Aladdin & Abu
27. Ken & Barbie
28. Sylvester & Tweety

42 Thursday

Page 43

MATH TIME

Remember:

Find the **area of a rectangle** by multiplying the height times the base. Find the **area of a right triangle** by multiplying the height by the base and dividing by 2.

Find the **area**.

1. 42
2. 16
3. 24
4. 20
5. 18

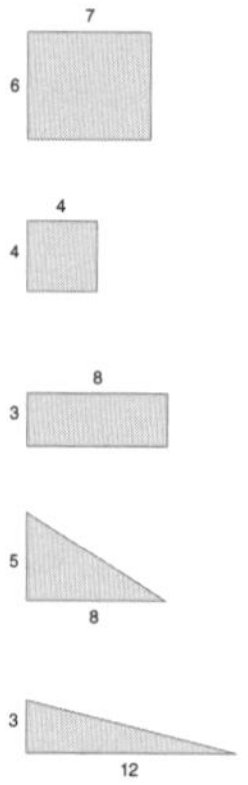

Find the **perimeter**.

1. 40
2. 30
3. 28
4. 31.4
5. 10.9

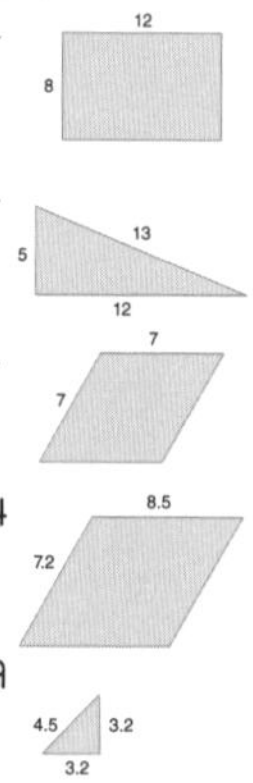

Friday WEEK 3 43

Page 44

Geography

South Asia

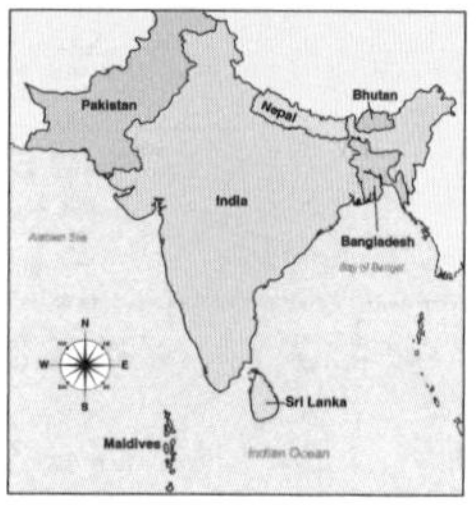

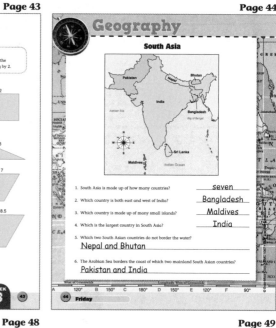

1. South Asia is made up of how many countries? seven
2. Which country is both east and west of India? Bangladesh
3. Which country is made up of many small islands? Maldives
4. Which is the largest country in South Asia? India
5. Which two South Asian countries do not border the water? Nepal and Bhutan
6. The Arabian Sea borders the coast of which two mainland South Asian countries? Pakistan and India

44 Friday

Page 47

Read It! Nonfiction

Read the article. Then answer the questions.

A Pyramid in Wyoming

When you think of pyramids, you probably picture one in Egypt or Mexico. Did you know that there is also a pyramid in the United States? Not many people are aware of it. You can find the pyramid, called the Ames Monument, off a quiet dirt road in the southeast corner of Wyoming.

Back in the 1800s, two brothers named Oliver and Oakes Ames worked with the Union Pacific Railroad to build train tracks that stretched across the country. This was a spectacular feat. However, Oakes was later charged with dishonest business practices, so the Ames brothers and the railroad company gained a bad reputation. After the Ames brothers died, the people who ran Union Pacific wanted to restore the company's public image. So they built a monument near Sherman, a quiet town at the highest point along the rail line. The builder used blocks of pink granite found in the area to construct the monument—a 60-foot pyramid. An artist added two 9-foot-tall carved portraits, one of each Ames brother.

At one time, train passengers traveling through the area could get off the train and view the pyramid up close. However, since then, the railroad tracks have been moved, and the town of Sherman no longer exists. Few people come to see the Ames Monument anymore, and the odd structure has fallen into disrepair. As a result, this pyramid may eventually vanish into history.

1. According to the passage, why did Union Pacific build the pyramid?
- Ⓐ to give passengers something to look at
- ● to improve the railroad's public image
- Ⓒ to impress the Ames brothers
- Ⓓ to compete with Egyptian pyramids

2. Which of these was an effect of Oakes Ames being charged with dishonest business practices?
- Ⓐ The Ames brothers moved to Sherman.
- Ⓑ People stopped taking the train.
- ● Union Pacific gained a bad reputation.
- Ⓓ An artist carved Oakes Ames's portrait.

3. What was probably the reason for choosing Sherman as the site of the monument?
- ● It was the highest point along the rail line.
- Ⓑ A lot of people lived there.
- Ⓒ The Ames brothers died there.
- Ⓓ Union Pacific headquarters was there.

4. What is the most likely reason that few people visit the pyramid today?
- ● Passenger trains no longer stop there.
- Ⓑ Union Pacific built a different monument.
- Ⓒ The Ames brothers died.
- Ⓓ The pyramid is in disrepair.

Monday WEEK 4 47

Page 48

Write It Right

Rewrite each sentence and correct the errors.

1. arent their no cookies left asked robert
   "Aren't there any cookies left?" asked Robert.
2. whos going to collect the five oclock male when its delivered
   Who's going to collect the five o'clock mail when it's delivered?
3. ive know idea what your talking about
   I've (*or* I have) no idea what you're talking about.
4. i comed to sea you but you wasnt there
   I came to see you, but you weren't there.

MATH TIME

Use the survey results to complete the circle graph and the key. Color each section of the graph a different color. Be sure the colors on your graph match the data and your key.

Survey Results

Cherry: 20 students
Cola: 70 students
Grape: 20 students
Lemon-Lime: 30 students
Orange: 10 students
Root Beer: 50 students

Favorite Flavor of Soda

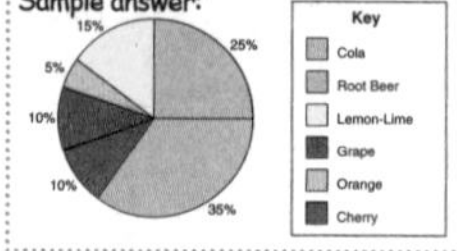

48 Monday

Page 49

SPELL IT

The /f/ sound can be spelled several ways:
f gh ph ff

Fill in the letter or letters that make the /f/ sound in the spelling words for the week. Then rewrite the word on the line next to it.

1. ph enomenal — phenomenal
2. chie f tain — chieftain
3. f lexible — flexible
4. sym ph ony — symphony
5. am ph ibian — amphibian
6. tou gh est — toughest
7. pam ph let — pamphlet
8. cou gh ing — coughing
9. twel f th — twelfth
10. f antasy — fantasy
11. e ff icient — efficient
12. ty ph oid — typhoid

In My Own Words

Finish this story: *Max found the end of the rainbow, but there was no pot of gold. Instead he found...*

Sample answer:
Instead he found an old man sitting peacefully.
"Do you know where the pot of gold is?" asked Max.
The old man chuckled. Max was not the first person to ask him that question.
"Why, what would you do with the gold if I told you where it is?" the man grinned.
Max pictured a new bike, new computer, and new hockey equipment. But then something in the old man's face made Max think about his own grandfather.
"I would give it to my grandpa," Max replied.
The old man smiled and presented Max with the gold.

Tuesday WEEK 4 49

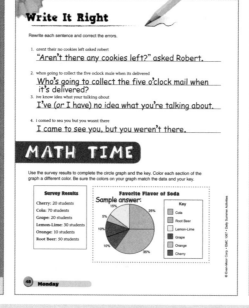

LANGUAGE LINES

Clipped words are shortened forms of longer words or phrases.
ad = advertisement

Write the clipped word that comes from each underlined word.

1. After class, Joe went back to his <u>dormitory</u>. — **dorm**
2. Mom has her final <u>examination</u> on Friday. — **exam**
3. The scientist spends all day in her <u>laboratory</u>. — **lab**
4. Chris's teacher found a <u>typographical</u> error in his report. — **typo**
5. Esteban had to wear a <u>tuxedo</u> to the wedding. — **tux**
6. The boss sent a <u>memorandum</u> about the meeting. — **memo**
7. The college <u>graduate</u> applied for several jobs. — **grad**
8. A <u>limousine</u> took the actor to the movie premiere. — **limo**

MATH TIME

Solve the word problem about probability.

There is a bag with 18 colored marbles inside. There are 6 white marbles, 2 green marbles, 1 red marble, and 9 blue marbles. If one marble is selected at random, what is the probability that it will be one of the following colors?

1. green: **1 in 9**   3. white: **1 in 3**
2. blue: **1 in 2**   4. red: **1 in 18**

Read It! Fiction

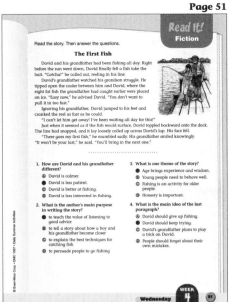

Read the story. Then answer the questions.

The First Fish

David and his grandfather had been fishing all day. Right before the sun went down, David felt a fish take the bait. "Gotcha!" he called out, reeling in his line.

David's grandfather watched his grandson struggle. He tipped open the cooler between him and David, where the eight fat fish the grandfather had caught earlier were placed on ice. "Easy now," he advised David. "You don't want to pull it in too fast."

Ignoring his grandfather, David jumped to his feet and cranked the reel as fast as he could.

"I can't let him get away! I've been waiting all day for this!" Just when it seemed as if the fish would surface, David toppled backward onto the dock. The line had snapped, and it lay loosely coiled up across David's lap. His face fell.

"There goes my first fish," he mumbled sadly. His grandfather smiled knowingly.

"It won't be your last," he said. "You'll bring in the next one."

1. How are David and his grandfather different?
ⓐ David is calmer.
ⓑ David is less patient.
ⓒ David is better at fishing.
ⓓ David is less interested in fishing.

2. What is the author's main purpose in writing the story?
ⓐ to teach the value of listening to good advice
ⓑ to tell a story about how a boy and his grandfather become closer
ⓒ to explain the best techniques for catching fish
ⓓ to persuade people to go fishing

3. What is one theme of the story?
ⓐ Age brings experience and wisdom.
ⓑ Young people need to behave well.
ⓒ Fishing is an activity for older people.
ⓓ Honesty is important.

4. What is the main idea of the last paragraph?
ⓐ David should give up fishing.
ⓑ David should keep trying.
ⓒ David's grandfather plans to play a trick on David.
ⓓ People should forget about their own mistakes.

Vo·cab·u·lar·y

Many English words originally came from Greek and Latin roots. Roots are word parts that form the base of words and can give clues to the words' meanings.

terr = land (<u>territory</u>)   therm = heat (<u>thermos</u>)
aqua/aqui = water (<u>aquarium</u>)   chron = time (<u>chronological</u>)

Write each word from the box under its correct definition in the chart below. Use a dictionary if necessary.

territory · terrace · terrain · thermos · aquarium · aquifer · chronic · aquamarine · thermostat · chronicle · thermometer · chronology

terr	therm	aqua/aqui	chron
an area of land that belongs to someone or something:	measures someone's temperature:	a sea-like, blue-green color:	lasting for a long time, or repeatedly:
territory	thermometer	aquamarine	chronic
an outdoor sitting area:	a container to keep liquids warm or cold:	where fish live indoors:	a list of events arranged in time order:
terrace	thermos	aquarium	chronicle
the natural features of land or ground:	raises or lowers the heat in your home:	an underground layer of rock containing water:	the science of recording events by date:
terrain	thermostat	aquifer	chronology

LANGUAGE LINES

A linking verb links the subject to a predicate noun or a predicate adjective.
Linking verbs: am are is was were can be will be

Circle the linking verb in each sentence. Write the predicate noun or predicate adjective on the line. The first one has been done for you.

1. Franklin (is) our hometown. — hometown
2. My mother's sisters (are) my aunts. — **aunts**
3. Some family stories (can be) funny. — **funny**
4. The potato salad (was) quite delicious. — **delicious**
5. The family reunion (will be) an important event. — **event**
6. That spinach salad (is) bright green! — **green**
7. (am) so happy for the winner. — **happy**
8. Robin wishes Tony and Katie (were) her partners. — **partners**

In My Own Words

Imagine that there is suddenly no gravity on Earth! Describe what you see happening around you.

Sample answer:
First, the lightest objects begin to float. Leaves, feathers, and cotton balls rise into the air. Next, dishes, rocks, and books start to hover. Suddenly, I am lifted off my feet, and the furniture around me leaves the ground. Soon everything that's not secured down is rising, rising ever higher into the atmosphere.

Mind Jigglers

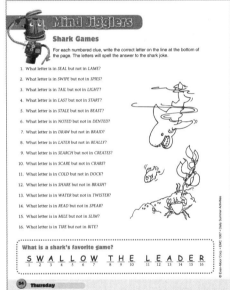

Shark Games

For each numbered clue, write the correct letter on the line at the bottom of the page. The letters will spell the answer to the shark joke.

1. What letter is in SEAL but not in LAME?
2. What letter is in SWIPE but not in SPIES?
3. What letter is in TAIL but not in LIGHT?
4. What letter is in LAST but not in START?
5. What letter is in STALE but not in BEAST?
6. What letter is in NOTED but not in DENTED?
7. What letter is in DRAW but not in BRAID?
8. What letter is in LATER but not in REALLY?
9. What letter is in SEARCH but not in CREATES?
10. What letter is in SCARE but not in CRABS?
11. What letter is in COLD but not in DOCK?
12. What letter is in SHARE but not in BRASH?
13. What letter is in WATER but not in TWISTER?
14. What letter is in READ but not in SPEAR?
15. What letter is in MILE but not in SLIM?
16. What letter is in TIRE but not in BITE?

What is a shark's favorite game?
S W A L L O W T H E L E A D E R
1 2 3 4 5 6 7 8 9 10 11 12 13 14 15 16

MATH TIME

Least Common Multiple

To solve the riddle, find the Least Common Multiple (LCM) for each set of numbers. Then write the corresponding letter on the line above the LCM. The letters will spell out the solution to the riddle at the bottom of the page.

Remember:
The Least Common Multiple (LCM) of two or more numbers is the smallest multiple that the numbers have in common.
The LCM of 4 and 5 is 20.
The LCM of 2 and 7 is 14.

1. LCM of 2 and 4 = **4** (A)
2. LCM of 5 and 6 = **30** (E)
3. LCM of 3 and 4 = **12** (W)
4. LCM of 4 and 5 = **20** (S)
5. LCM of 6 and 9 = **18** (E)
6. LCM of 5 and 3 = **15** (S)
7. LCM of 7 and 3 = **21** (T)
8. LCM of 22 and 4 = **44** (T)
9. LCM of 16 and 3 = **48** (T)
10. LCM of 6 and 8 = **24** (E)
11. LCM of 10 and 8 = **40** (W)

What did the bird buy at the mall?
A S W E E T T W E E T
4 15 40 12 30 44 21 24 20 18 48

Geography

The Great Lakes

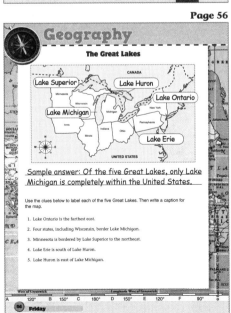

Sample answer: Of the five Great Lakes, only Lake Michigan is completely within the United States.

Use the clues below to label each of the five Great Lakes. Then write a caption for the map.

1. Lake Ontario is the farthest east.
2. Four states, including Wisconsin, border Lake Michigan.
3. Minnesota is bordered by Lake Superior to the northeast.
4. Lake Erie is south of Lake Huron.
5. Lake Huron is east of Lake Michigan.

Read It! Fiction

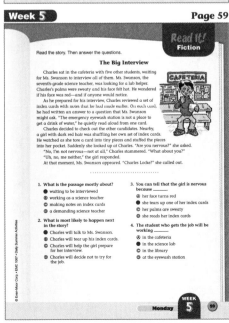

Read the story. Then answer the questions.

The Big Interview

Charles sat in the cafeteria with five other students, waiting for Ms. Swanson to interview all of them. Ms. Swanson, the seventh-grade science teacher, was looking for a lab helper. Charles's palms were sweaty and his face felt hot. He wondered if his face was red—and if anyone would notice.

As he prepared for his interview, Charles reviewed a set of index cards with notes that he had made earlier. On each card, he had written an answer to a question that Ms. Swanson might ask. "The emergency eyewash station is not a place to get a drink of water," he quietly read aloud from one card.

Charles decided to check out the other candidates. Nearby, a girl with dark red hair was shuffling her own set of index cards. He watched as she tore a card into tiny pieces and stuffed the pieces into her pocket. Suddenly she looked up at Charles. "Are you nervous?" she asked.

"No, I'm not nervous—not at all," Charles stammered. "What about you?"

"Uh, no, me neither," the girl responded.

At that moment, Ms. Swanson appeared. "Charles Locke?" she called out.

1. What is the passage mostly about?
ⓐ waiting to be interviewed
ⓑ working as a science teacher
ⓒ making notes on index cards
ⓓ a demanding science teacher

2. What is most likely to happen next in the story?
ⓐ Charles will talk to Ms. Swanson.
ⓑ Charles will tear up his index cards.
ⓒ Charles will help the girl prepare for her interview.
ⓓ Charles will decide not to try for the job.

3. You can tell that the girl is nervous because—
ⓐ her face turns red
ⓑ she tears up one of her index cards
ⓒ her palms are sweaty
ⓓ she reads her index cards

4. The student who gets the job will be working—
ⓐ in the cafeteria
ⓑ in the science lab
ⓒ in the library
ⓓ at the eyewash station

Write It Right

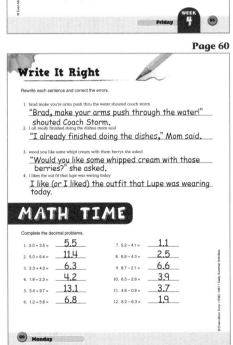

Rewrite each sentence and correct the errors.

1. brad make you're arms push thru the water shouted coach storm
"Brad, make your arms push through the water!" shouted Coach Storm.

2. I all ready finished doing the dishus mom said
"I already finished doing the dishes," Mom said.

3. wood you like some whipt cream with them berrys she asked
"Would you like some whipped cream with those berries?" she asked.

4. I likes the out fit that lupe was wering today
I like (or I liked) the outfit that Lupe was wearing today.

MATH TIME

Complete the decimal problems.

1. 2.0 + 3.5 = **5.5**
2. 5.0 + 6.4 = **11.4**
3. 2.3 + 4.0 = **6.3**
4. 1.9 + 2.3 = **4.2**
5. 3.4 + 9.7 = **13.1**
6. 1.2 + 5.6 = **6.8**
7. 5.2 − 4.1 = **1.1**
8. 6.8 − 4.3 = **2.5**
9. 8.7 − 2.1 = **6.6**
10. 6.5 − 2.6 = **3.9**
11. 4.6 − 0.9 = **3.7**
12. 8.2 − 6.3 = **1.9**

Answer Key 133

Page 61

SPELL IT

Some **prefixes** indicate numbers or amounts.
uni-: one **bi-**: two **tri-**: three **semi-**: half or partial **cent-**: hundred

Complete the spelling words for the week by filling in the correct prefixes.

1. semi **annual:** twice a year
2. cent **ipede:** a creature with many legs (literally: hundred legs)
3. bi **lingual:** speaking two languages
4. tri **ad:** a group of three
5. uni **fy:** to bring together as one
6. cent **ennial:** a hundredth anniversary
7. bi **pedal:** having two feet
8. tri **athlon:** a three-part athletic event
9. uni **que:** unlike any other; being the only one
10. tri **ceps:** muscles with three points of attachment
11. semi **circle:** half a circle
12. bi **noculars:** using both eyes

In My Own Words

Use some of your spelling words to write a funny or factual sentence about a centipede.

Sample answer:
Unlike humans, who are bipedal, centipedes are unique creatures with 100 legs.

Page 62

LANGUAGE LINES

Comparative adjectives use -er to compare two people, places, things, or ideas.
Superlative adjectives use -est to compare three or more people, places, things, or ideas.

Circle the correct form of the adjective to complete each sentence. On the line, write *C* for comparative or *S* for superlative to identify the type of adjective.

1. The Rocky Mountains are C than the Appalachians.	(taller)	tallest
2. The Mississippi is the S river and the most famous.	mightier	(mightiest)
3. Chicago is the S city in the country, according to its nickname.	windier	(windiest)
4. I visited New York City, and it was C than where I live.	(noisier)	noisiest
5. Florida, the "Sunshine State," must be C than Illinois.	(sunnier)	sunniest
6. Alaska must be the S of all states, being so far north.	colder	(coldest)
7. Many places could claim to be the S in America.	prettier	(prettiest)
8. I would like to live in the place that is the S.	friendlier	(friendliest)

MATH TIME

Solve the word problems about books.

1. Patricia bought a book at the bookstore. She got $2.25 from her mom, $3.25 from her dad, and $4.00 from her older sister to buy the book. Patricia had to kick in the last $2.49. How much did the book cost?

Answer: $11.99

2. How much would Patricia's book cost if it were 25% off? Round to the nearest cent.

Answer: $8.99

Page 63

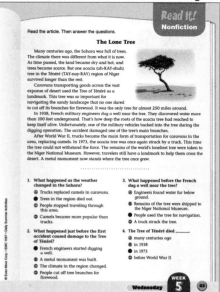

Read It! Nonfiction

Read the article. Then answer the questions.

The Lone Tree

Many centuries ago, the Sahara was full of trees. The climate there was different from what it is now. As time passed, the land became dry and hot, and trees became scarce. But one acacia (uh-KAY-shuh) tree in the Ténéré (TAY-nay-RAY) region of Niger survived longer than the rest.

Caravans transporting goods across the vast expanse of desert used the Tree of Ténéré as a landmark. This tree was so important for navigating the sandy landscape that no one dared to cut off its branches for firewood. It was the only tree for almost 250 miles around.

In 1938, French military engineers dug a well near the tree. They discovered water more than 100 feet underground. That's how deep the roots of the acacia tree had reached to keep itself alive. Unfortunately, one of the military vehicles backed into the tree during the digging operation. The accident damaged one of the tree's main branches.

After World War II, trucks became the main form of transportation for caravans in the area, replacing camels. In 1973, the acacia tree was once again struck by a truck. This time the tree could not withstand the force. The remains of the world's loneliest tree were taken to the Niger National Museum. However, travelers still have a landmark to help them cross the desert. A metal monument now stands where the tree once grew.

1. **What happened as the weather changed in the Sahara?**
   - (A) Trucks replaced camels in caravans.
   - ● Trees in the region died out.
   - (C) People stopped traveling through this area.
   - (D) Camels became more popular than trucks.
2. **What happened just before the first accident caused damage to the Tree of Ténéré?**
   - ● French engineers started digging a well.
   - (B) A metal monument was built.
   - (C) The climate in the region changed.
   - (D) People cut off tree branches for firewood.
3. **What happened before the French dug a well near the tree?**
   - (A) Engineers found water far below ground.
   - (B) Remains of the tree were shipped to the Niger National Museum.
   - ● People used the tree for navigation.
   - (D) A truck struck the tree.
4. **The Tree of Ténéré died _____.**
   - (A) many centuries ago
   - (B) in 1938
   - ● in 1973
   - (D) before World War II

Page 64

Vo•cab•u•lar•y

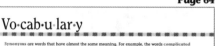

Synonyms are words that have almost the same meaning. For example, the words **complicated** and **complex** are synonyms.

This math puzzle is fairly complicated.
I hope I'll be able to solve this complex puzzle.

A. Use the words in the box to write a synonym for each word below. Use a dictionary if necessary.

remove glossy instruct persuasive
conclude humorous bewilder courageous

1. convincing persuasive
2. lustrous glossy
3. confound bewilder
4. terminate conclude
5. eliminate remove
6. witty humorous
7. valiant courageous
8. educate instruct

B. Complete each sentence with a synonym from Activity A.

1. Let's terminate (conclude) this lesson five minutes before lunchtime.
2. I brushed my cat until her fur looked lustrous (glossy).
3. This detergent will eliminate (remove) stains from your clothing.
4. The valiant (courageous) firefighter saved three people's lives.
5. Complicated science projects often confound (bewilder) me.
6. A convincing (persuasive) argument may change someone's mind.

Page 65

LANGUAGE LINES

You can correct run-on sentences by turning them into two sentences or by forming a compound or a complex sentence.

Compound sentence: Alejandro played soccer, and Lucas played baseball.
Complex sentence: When James came home, he started his homework.

Correct and rewrite each run-on sentence as directed.

1. Patty and I went to the shoe store we tried on lots of shoes.
   Two simple sentences: Patty and I went to the shoe store. We tried on lots of shoes.
2. We went to the card store, I needed a birthday card.
   Complex sentence: We went to the card store because I needed a birthday card.
3. Patty likes to try on clothes, I would rather try on shoes.
   Compound sentence: Patty likes to try on clothes, but I would rather try on shoes.

In My Own Words

Make a list of 10 words that describe you.

Sample answer:
1. smart
2. caring
3. adventurous
4. funny
5. thoughtful
6. kind
7. brave
8. scatterbrained
9. silly
10. charming

Page 66

Mind Jigglers

Water Works

A. See how quickly you can answer the questions below.

1. Where are six places you could find water in nature? Sample answers:
   ocean, river, clouds, lake, stream, ice
2. What are six things that you can put in water?
   fish, frogs, boats, turtles, flowers, surfboards
3. What are six things that you can use water for?
   drinking, doing laundry, cooking, watering plants, taking a shower, washing dishes

B. Your body is 70 percent water. A cup of water weighs about half a pound. About how many cups of water do you have in your body?

Sample answer:

Your weight: 90 pounds
Cups of water in your body: 31.5

C. There are 3 identical pitchers in a row. The first one has twice as much water in it as the third one. The second one has one-third the amount of water as the first one. Draw the amount of water in each pitcher.

Sample answer:

Page 67

MATH TIME

What's Your Range?

Remember:
Range is the difference between the greatest and the least number in a set of data.
Set: 21, 15, 27, 12, 20
27 – 12 = 15
Range: 15

Find the **range**.

1. 5, 7, 15, 8, 23, 8 — 18
2. 59, 48, 61, 61, 57, 42, 60, 53, 54 — 19
3. 23, 31, 45, 22, 62, 41, 26, 38 — 40

Remember:
Mean is the average of a set of data. Add the numbers, then divide the sum of the numbers by the number of addends.
Set: 21, 15, 27, 12, 20
21 + 15 + 27 + 12 + 20 = 95
95 ÷ 5 = 19
Mean: 19

Find the **mean**.

1. 19, 3, 7, 22, 5, 25 — 13.5
2. 13, 32, 6, 26, 30, 44, 12, 29 — 24
3. 61, 46, 23, 40, 39, 21, 32, 28 — 36.25

Remember:
Median is the middle number in a set of sequenced data.
Set: 21, 15, 27, 12, 20
12, 15, 20, 21, 27
Median: 20

Find the **median**.

1. 2, 6, 28, 9, 40, 9, 17 — 9
2. 56, 36, 43, 52, 59, 20, 70 — 52
3. 41, 19, 81, 80, 51, 57, 69, 15, 60 — 57

Remember:
Mode is the number that appears the most often in a set of data. Some sets have no mode.
Set: 21, 15, 27, 12, 20
There is no mode.

Find the **mode**.

1. 22, 22, 22, 22 — 22
2. 14, 12, 19, 13, 12, 13, 17, 12 — 12
3. 33, 31, 45, 92, 47, 86 — no mode

Page 68

Geography

Countries of Western Europe

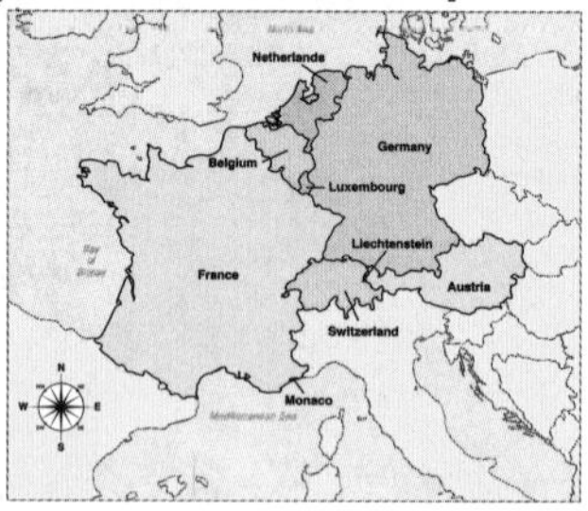

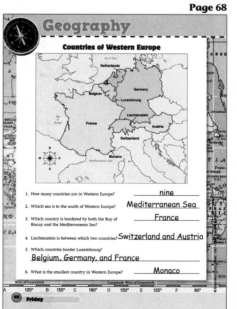

1. How many countries are in Western Europe? nine
2. Which sea is to the south of Western Europe? Mediterranean Sea
3. Which country is bordered by both the Bay of Biscay and the Mediterranean Sea? France
4. Liechtenstein is between which two countries? Switzerland and Austria
5. Which countries border Luxembourg? Belgium, Germany, and France
6. What is the smallest country in Western Europe? Monaco

Week 6

Page 71

Read It! Fiction

Read the story. Then answer the questions.

The Egg Drop

Marisol, Jack, and Ramon met after school to work on their group science project. Their assignment was to find a way to protect an egg from breaking as it was dropped from a two-story building. Marisol and Ramon were busy working with their materials, which included a pile of newspapers, some bubble wrap, and rubber bands. Marisol was tearing newspapers into strips and watching Jack doodle in a notebook. Finally, she couldn't stay quiet any longer.

"Jack, when are you going to help us?" she asked. "We need to get this project done today."

Ramon reached across the table for another rubber band to weave into the rubber mat he was trying to make. "Yeah, Jack," he said. "Could you put down your cartoons and help us?" Jack was a good friend, but he didn't seem to give science class the same attention that Ramon and Marisol did. His mind always seemed to be somewhere else—mainly in his notebook.

Jack looked up so slowly that Marisol and Ramon thought he may not have heard them at all. Then he turned the page toward them. Jack had sketched a diagram that showed an egg in the center of a layer of newspaper and bubble wrap. The egg had been wrapped with several rubber bands, which crisscrossed each other to make a thick layer of padding. Marisol and Ramon were impressed.

"I was just brainstorming," Jack said. "Do you think it'll work?"

1. **What do the three students have in common?**
   - (A) They like to draw cartoons.
   - ● They are working on the same project.
   - (C) They are easily distracted.
   - (D) They do not want to use rubber bands.
2. **How is Jack's way of working on the project different from that of his partners?**
   - (A) He doesn't work as hard as they do.
   - ● He sketches his ideas first.
   - (C) He doesn't care if the egg breaks.
   - (D) He wants to spend more time on it.
3. **How is Jack's plan different from Ramon's?**
   - (A) It uses different materials.
   - (B) It will be more difficult to do.
   - (C) It will keep the egg from breaking.
   - ● It uses rubber bands in a different way.
4. **What do Marisol and Ramon probably think at the end of the story?**
   - (A) They decide their ideas are not very good.
   - (B) They think they need a sketch to succeed.
   - (C) They agree they do not need Jack's help.
   - ● They realize Jack has been working the whole time.

Write It Right

Rewrite each sentence and correct the errors.

1. josh torie and maddie went to disney world

Josh, Torie, and Maddie went to Disney World.

2. they road on three rides called space mountain rock 'n' roller coaster and test track

They rode on three rides called Space Mountain, Rock 'n' Roller Coaster, and Test Track.

3. theyre favorite part were watching the firework's at epcot center

Their favorite part was watching the fireworks at Epcot Center.

MATH TIME

Solve the multiplication and division problems.

1. 2.2 × 3.0 = **6.6**
2. 8.6 × 2.0 = **17.2**
3. 1.0 × 5.3 = **5.3**
4. 5.0 × 2.3 = **11.5**
5. 6.9 × 6.5 = **44.85**
6. 10.25 × 11.3 = **115.825**
7. 9.1 ÷ 7.0 = **1.3**
8. 4.5 ÷ 1.8 = **2.5**
9. 5.39 ÷ 1.1 = **4.9**
10. 23.0 ÷ 5.0 = **4.6**
11. 17.836 ÷ 3.43 = **5.2**
12. 12.015 ÷ 1.5 = **8.01**

72 | Monday

SPELLIT

Most plural nouns are formed by adding –s or –es. Sometimes you must also change the last letter of the singular noun before adding –s or –es.

Change each singular noun to its plural form to make the spelling words for the week.

1. half — **halves**
2. variety — **varieties**
3. boundary — **boundaries**
4. journey — **journeys**
5. belief — **beliefs**
6. passerby — **passersby**
7. echo — **echoes**
8. schedule — **schedules**
9. thief — **thieves**
10. substance — **substances**
11. tomato — **tomatoes**
12. mosquito — **mosquitoes**

In My Own Words

An example of a tongue twister is "Sister Susie sells seashells by the seashore." Write two of your own tongue twisters.

Sample answers:
Roberta ran rings around the Roman ruins.

Three thousand tricky tongue twisters trip thrillingly off the tongue.

Tuesday | WEEK 6 | 73

LANGUAGE LINES

The present progressive tense of a verb shows that an action is in progress. The action is happening now and will continue for a period of time.

Underline the present progressive verb in each sentence. The first one has been done for you.

1. Shoppers are waiting for the store to open.
2. The manager is unlocking the door.
3. Everyone is hoping for a bargain.
4. I am searching for shoes for the party.
5. Chris is unfolding a green sweater.
6. My parents are paying for these shoes.

MATH TIME

Complete the table below so that each row shows three representations of the same value. The first row has been done for you.

Fraction	Decimal	Percent
1/4	0.25	25%
1/2	0.5	50%
7/10	0.7	70%
3/4	0.75	75%
4/5	0.8	80%
	0.4	40%

74 | Tuesday

Read It! Nonfiction

Read the article. Then answer the questions.

The Loneliest Island

In the middle of the frigid South Atlantic Ocean, one island stands alone. It lies near Antarctica. But it is far enough away that early explorers had difficulty finding it. At about four miles long, the island is covered with glaciers. It is home to an inactive volcano and huge amounts of ice. The island is cold year-round, with an average temperature of about 29°F. The steep cliffs that surround the island make sea landings almost impossible. This is Bouvet Island, the loneliest island in the world.

A French explorer discovered Bouvet Island in 1739, but the island was so difficult to approach that nobody set foot on it for nearly a hundred years. No people live on Bouvet Island, and little vegetation grows there. Seals come and go, but they haven't seen humans since the mid- to late-20th century, when seal hunting and whaling stopped in the area.

In recent years, Bouvet Island has had a little more contact with the world. Norway, which claimed the island in 1928, set up an unmanned weather station there in 1977. Today, this quiet island near the South Pole sends weather data to a satellite, which transmits the information to researchers in Norway. Scientists learn more every day about the island and its surroundings. Meanwhile, Bouvet Island stays strong and silent in the harsh climate.

1. What could you correctly predict from the title of the article?
   - The island is very small.
   - No one lives on the island.
   - The passage is about Antarctica.
   - ● Only lonely people live on the island.

2. What can you correctly predict about Bouvet Island after reading the first sentence?
   - ● It is cold most of the year.
   - It is volcanic.
   - Norway claimed it in 1928.
   - It is near the North Pole.

3. What can you conclude after reading that steep cliffs surround the island?
   - The island is covered in glaciers.
   - Explorers cannot find the island.
   - ● There is nowhere to dock a boat on the island.
   - The island is near the South Pole.

4. After scientists receive data from the weather station, they will most likely
   - try to determine the island's location
   - study weather patterns on the island
   - track the movements of seals
   - ● send the information to a satellite

Wednesday | WEEK 6 | 75

Vo·cab·u·lar·y

Antonyms are words that have opposite meanings.

Doubt is an antonym of certainty.
Knowledge is an antonym of ignorance.

Write each word from the box under its correct antonym in the grid to complete a row, column, or diagonal. Circle the winning four-in-a-row. Use a dictionary if necessary.

deny	active	insult	definite
humble	flexible	opponent	taper

lively	sure	compliment	teammate
		insult	**opponent**
immature	vague	rigid	confirm
	definite	**flexible**	**deny**
limber	modest	refuse	arrogant
			humble
offend	widen	tragic	idle
	taper		**active**

78 | Wednesday

LANGUAGE LINES

An adverb can modify a verb, an adjective, or another adverb. Adverbs can tell how, where, when, and to what extent.

Underline the adverb and draw an arrow to the word it modifies. The first one has been done for you.

1. "There you are!" cried Alex's mother.
2. His mother anxiously asked him where he'd been.
3. "I missed the bus and had to walk here," Alex replied.
4. "You have an orthodontist appointment tomorrow," Alex's mother said.
5. "That means you have to leave school early," she continued.
6. "I'll be very happy when my braces are removed," Alex said.
7. "Me, too," his mother replied tiredly.

In My Own Words

Make a list of five of your favorite activities and explain why you like them.

Sample answers:
1. softball, because I love the sound the bat makes when it connects with the ball
2. listening to music, because I enjoy singing along
3. playing video games, because I like being different characters and living out their stories
4. reading, because it stirs my imagination
5. hiking, because I like being outdoors and

Thursday | WEEK 6 | 77

Mind Jigglers

Hink Pinks and Hinky Pinkies

A. Write two rhyming words to match each description. For example, a healthy chime is a well bell, and a thorny little instrument is a thistle whistle.

ill baby chicken	**sick chick**
chubby kitty	**fat cat**
rodent dwelling	**mouse house**
shark's plate	**fish dish**
bloody tale	**gory story**
rabbit seat	**hare chair**
idle flower	**lazy daisy**
wet puppy	**soggy doggy**
grumpy taxi driver	**crabby cabby**
timid bug	**shy fly**
intelligent graph	**smart chart**
unkind adolescent	**mean teen**
bad breakfast item	**awful waffle**
funny female horse	**silly filly**
phony serpent	**fake snake**
frightening pet bird	**scary canary**
monster university	**ghoul school**
upbeat Thanksgiving bird	**perky turkey**
reptilian magician	**lizard wizard**

B. Now make up some of your own.

Sample answers:
a married rodent:
mouse spouse
a young cat in love:
smitten kitten
an anxious snake:
hyper viper

78 | Thursday

MATH TIME

Outer Planets

What are the planets Jupiter, Saturn, Uranus, and Neptune called? To find the answer to this question, solve each problem on the right. Then write the corresponding letter on the line above the correct number. The letters will spell out the answer.

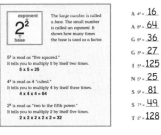

The large number is called a base. The small number is called an exponent. It shows how many times the base is used as a factor.

5^2 is read as "five squared."
It tells you to multiply 5 by itself two times.
$5 \times 5 = 25$

4^3 is read as 4 "cubed."
It tells you to multiply 4 by itself three times.
$4 \times 4 \times 4 = 64$

2^5 is read as "two to the fifth power."
It tells you to multiply 2 by itself five times.
$2 \times 2 \times 2 \times 2 \times 2 = 32$

A $4^2 =$ **16**
A $8^2 =$ **64**
G $6^2 =$ **36**
G $3^3 =$ **27**
I $5^3 =$ **125**
N $5^2 =$ **25**
S $9^2 =$ **81**
S $7^2 =$ **49**
T $2^7 =$ **128**

$\underset{36}{G}\ \underset{64}{A}\ \underset{81}{S}$

$\underset{27}{G}\ \underset{125}{I}\ \underset{16}{A}\ \underset{25}{N}\ \underset{128}{T}\ \underset{49}{S}$

Friday | WEEK 6 | 79

Geography

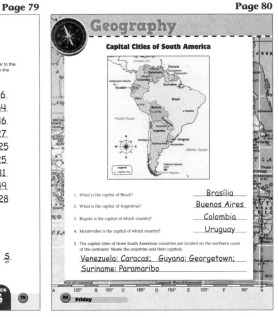

Capital Cities of South America

1. What is the capital of Brazil? — **Brasília**
2. What is the capital of Argentina? — **Buenos Aires**
3. Bogotá is the capital of which country? — **Colombia**
4. Montevideo is the capital of which country? — **Uruguay**
5. The capital cities of three South American countries are located on the northern coast of the continent. Name the countries and their capitals.

Venezuela: Caracas; Guyana: Georgetown; Suriname: Paramaribo

80 | Friday

Answer Key | **135**

Page 83

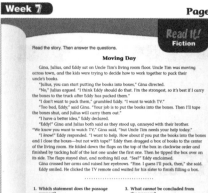

Read It! Fiction

Read the story. Then answer the questions.

Moving Day

Gina, Julius, and Eddy sat on Uncle Tim's living room floor. Uncle Tim was moving across town, and the kids were trying to decide how to work together to pack their uncle's books.

"Julius, you can start putting the books into boxes," Gina directed.

"No," Julius argued. "I think Eddy should do that. I'm the strongest, so it's best if I carry the boxes to the truck after Eddy has packed them."

"I don't want to pack them," grumbled Eddy. "I want to watch TV."

"Too bad, Eddy," said Gina. "Your job is to put the books into the boxes. Then I'll tape the boxes shut, and Julius will carry them out."

"I have a better idea," Eddy declared.

"Eddy!" Gina and Julius both said as they stood up, annoyed with their brother. "We know you want to watch TV," Gina said, "but Uncle Tim needs your help today."

"I *know*!" Eddy responded. "I want to help. How about if you put the books into the boxes and I close the boxes—but not with tape?" Eddy then dragged a box of books to the center of the living room. He folded down the flaps on the top of the box in clockwise order and finished by tucking half of the last one under the first one. Then he tipped the box over on its side. The flaps stayed shut, and nothing fell out. "See?" Eddy exclaimed.

Gina crossed her arms and raised her eyebrows. "Fine. I guess I'll pack, then," she said. Eddy smiled. He clicked the TV remote and waited for his sister to finish filling a box.

1. **Which statement does the passage support?**
   - Ⓐ Julius, Gina, and Eddy cannot find a way to work together.
   - Ⓑ Eddy is more excited to help Uncle Tim than Gina is.
   - ● Julius is more eager to carry the boxes than Gina is.
   - Ⓓ Uncle Tim has a better TV than the kids do.
2. **Gina and Julius are both ______**
   - Ⓐ reading Uncle Tim's books
   - Ⓑ ready to watch TV instead of work
   - ● good at giving orders
   - Ⓓ eager to carry the boxes
3. **What *cannot* be concluded from the passage?**
   - Ⓐ The kids want to help their uncle.
   - ● Everyone wants to pack the boxes.
   - Ⓒ Eddy is clever.
   - Ⓓ Julius is strong.
4. **Why is Eddy smiling at the end of the story?**
   - ● He can watch TV while Gina fills the boxes.
   - Ⓑ He can watch TV instead of helping.
   - Ⓒ He likes his uncle's books.
   - Ⓓ He is glad that he does not have to use tape.

Monday WEEK 7 83

Page 84

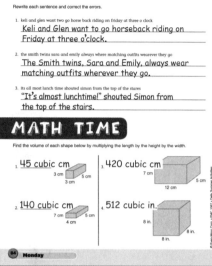

Write It Right

Rewrite each sentence and correct the errors.

1. keli and glen want two go horse back riding on friday at three o clock
   Keli and Glen want to go horseback riding on Friday at three o'clock.
2. the smith twins sara and emily always where matching outfits wearever they go
   The Smith twins, Sara and Emily, always wear matching outfits wherever they go.
3. its all most lunch time shouted simon from the top of the stares
   "It's almost lunchtime!" shouted Simon from the top of the stairs.

MATH TIME

Find the volume of each shape below by multiplying the length by the height by the width.

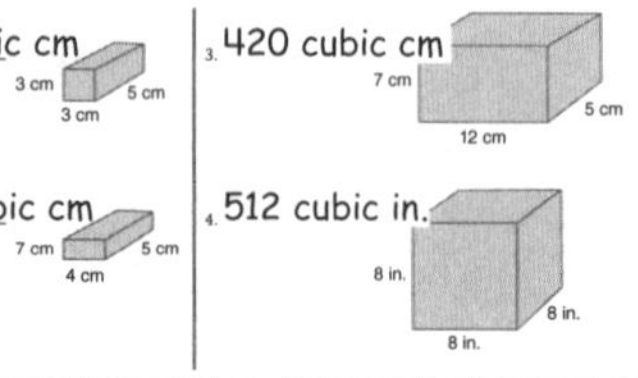

3 cm
5 cm
3 cm
7 cm
12 cm
5 cm
7 cm
5 cm
4 cm
8 in.
8 in.
8 in.

1. 45 cubic cm
2. 140 cubic cm
3. 420 cubic cm
4. 512 cubic in.

84 Monday

Page 85

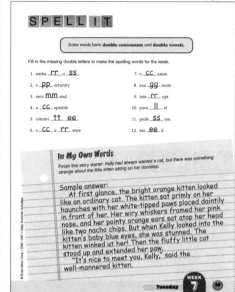

SPELL IT

Some words have **double consonants** and **double vowels.**

Fill in the missing double letters to make the spelling words for the week.

1. emba rr a ss
2. o pp ortunity
3. reco mm end
4. a cc eptable
5. commi tt ee
6. o cc u rr ence
7. o cc asion
8. exa gg erate
9. inte rr upt
10. para ll el
11. profe ss ion
12. exc ee d

In My Own Words

Finish this story starter: *Kelly had always wanted a cat, but there was something strange about the little kitten sitting on her doorstep.*

Sample answer:
At first glance, the bright orange kitten looked like an ordinary cat. The kitten sat primly on her haunches with her white-tipped paws placed daintily in front of her. Her wiry whiskers framed her pink nose, and her pointy orange ears sat atop her head like two nacho chips. But when Kelly looked into the kitten's baby blue eyes, she was stunned. The kitten winked at her! Then the fluffy little cat stood up and extended her paw.
"It's nice to meet you, Kelly," said the well-mannered kitten.

Tuesday WEEK 7 85

Page 86

LANGUAGE LINES

A clause is a group of related words that has its own subject and predicate. An independent clause can stand alone as a complete sentence, while a dependent clause cannot.

Circle whether the underlined group of words is an *independent clause* or a *dependent clause.*

1. Because birds are popular, pet stores carry a variety of them. — independent / **(dependent)**
2. They are popular because they are colorful and smart. — **(independent)** / dependent
3. I love my canary because of its yellow feathers. — **(independent)** / dependent
4. He sings when I uncover the cage in the morning. — independent / **(dependent)**
5. I bought my bird at the pet store in the mall. — **(independent)** / dependent
6. When he needs to eat, I fill his cup with seeds. — **(independent)** / dependent

MATH TIME

Look at each value in the box. Locate the value on the number line and write the corresponding letter above the line. The letters will spell out the solution to the riddle.

What goes up when rain comes down?

20 A	−14 N	15 L	2 R	13 L
−7 U	8 E	−18 A	0 B	−3 M

A N U M B R E L L A
−20 −15 −10 −5 0 5 10 15 20

86 Tuesday

Page 87

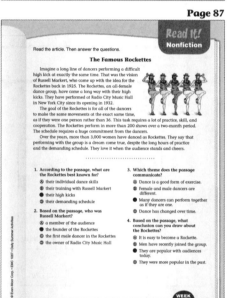

Read It! Nonfiction

Read the article. Then answer the questions.

The Famous Rockettes

Imagine a long line of dancers performing a difficult high kick at exactly the same time. That was the vision of Russell Markert, who came up with the idea for the Rockettes back in 1925. The Rockettes, an all-female dance group, have come a long way with their high kicks. They have performed at Radio City Music Hall in New York City since its opening in 1932.

The goal of the Rockettes is for all of the dancers to make the same movements at the exact same time, as if they were one person rather than 36. This task requires a lot of practice, skill, and cooperation. The Rockettes perform in more than 200 shows over a two-month period. The schedule requires a huge commitment from the dancers.

Over the years, more than 3,000 women have danced as Rockettes. They say that performing with the group is a dream come true, despite the long hours of practice and the demanding schedule. They love it when the audience stands and cheers.

1. **According to the passage, what are the Rockettes best known for?**
   - Ⓐ their individual dance skills
   - Ⓑ their training with Russell Markert
   - ● their high kicks
   - Ⓓ their demanding schedule
2. **Based on the passage, who was Russell Markert?**
   - Ⓐ a member of the audience
   - ● the founder of the Rockettes
   - Ⓒ the first male dancer in the Rockettes
   - Ⓓ the owner of Radio City Music Hall
3. **Which theme does the passage communicate?**
   - Ⓐ Dance is a good form of exercise.
   - Ⓑ Female and male dancers are different.
   - ● Many dancers can perform together as if they are one.
   - Ⓓ Dance has changed over time.
4. **Based on the passage, what conclusion can you draw about the Rockettes?**
   - Ⓐ It is easy to become a Rockette.
   - Ⓑ Men have recently joined the group.
   - ● They are popular with audiences today.
   - Ⓓ They were more popular in the past.

Wednesday WEEK 7 87

Page 88

Vo•cab•u•lar•y

A **prefix** is a word part that comes at the beginning of a word and affects its meaning.

The prefixes **em–** and **en–** mean "in" or "into."
The prefix **inter–** means "between."
The prefix **trans–** means "across."

A. Add the prefix **em–, en–, inter–,** or **trans–** to each word or word part in the box. The words you form will answer the clues below. Write the words next to the correct clues. Use a dictionary if necessary.

em brace	inter vene	en danger	en courage
trans mit	trans portation	inter mission	inter continental

1. something that can carry you across distances — transportation
2. something between two acts in a play — intermission
3. to take someone into your arms — embrace
4. to send a message across a distance — transmit
5. to put in harm's way — endanger
6. to give support and confidence — encourage
7. between two or more countries — intercontinental
8. to come between two people — intervene

B. Use at least two of the words from Activity A in a sentence.

Sample answer: With a swift embrace backstage during intermission, Arianna's parents encourage her to go out and finish the show.

88 Wednesday

Page 89

LANGUAGE LINES

A prepositional phrase is a group of words that begins with a preposition and ends with a noun or pronoun. This noun or pronoun is called the object of the preposition.

Write the prepositional phrase from the box to complete each sentence. Circle the preposition. Then draw a line under the object of the preposition.

around the room	during the meal	to the dinner	at school
after the messy diners	for our class trip	onto warm plates	

1. The sixth grade had a spaghetti dinner (at) school.
2. We wanted to raise money (for) our class trip.
3. About 60 people came (to) the dinner.
4. We put up twinkling lights (around) the room so it would look special.
5. We played music (during) the meal to be festive.
6. Some students' job was to dish out the spaghetti (onto) warm plates.
7. Other students cleared the tables and cleaned up (after) the messy diners.

In My Own Words

What is the most important attribute of a friend? Why is this important to you?

Sample answer:
The most important attribute of a friend is a good sense of humor. Having fun and making each other laugh is important because it helps you get each other through tough times and keeps you from fighting over silly things.

Thursday WEEK 7 89

Page 90

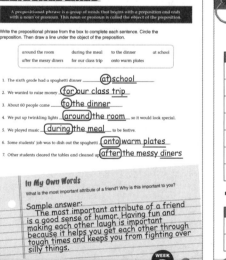

Mind Jigglers

School Lunch

A. All of the children listed below are very picky about the lunches they eat at school. All of the items in each child's lunch must start with the same letter as his or her name. Fill in the chart to make each child a lunch.

Sample answers:

Name	Main Dish	Fruit or Veggie	Snack or Dessert	Drink
Sarah	salad	strawberries	shortcake	soda
Pete	pasta	pears	popcorn	pineapple juice
Carlos	chicken	celery	chips	cider
Trina	tacos	tomatoes	tapioca pudding	tea
Michael	macaroni and cheese	melon	marshmallows	milk
Fiona	falafel	figs	frozen yogurt	fruit punch
Gina	garden burger	green beans	granola	ginger ale

B. Garret and Jennifer both have double letters in their names. Can you make a different lunch for each kid, using only foods with double letters?

Name	Main Dish	Fruit or Veggie	Snack or Dessert	Drink
Garrett	pizza	zucchini	jello	coffee
Jennifer	sloppy joes	cherries	carrot cake	apple juice

90 Thursday

Page 91

MATH TIME

New Deli Directions

The letters on the grid below represent different buildings in the town of New Deli. Use the grid to answer the questions.

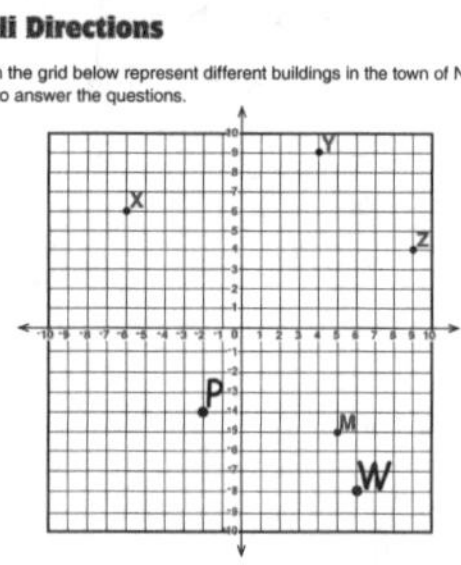

X
Y
Z
P
M
W

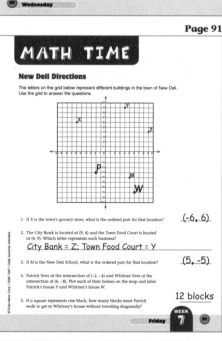

1. If *X* is the town's grocery store, what is the ordered pair for that location? (−6, 6)
2. The City Bank is located at (9, 4) and the Town Food Court is located at (4, 9). Which letter represents each business?
   City Bank = Z; Town Food Court = Y
3. If *M* is the New Deli School, what is the ordered pair for that location? (5, −5)
4. Patrick lives at the intersection of (−2, −4) and Whitney lives at the intersection of (6, −8). Plot each of their homes on the map and label Patrick's house *P* and Whitney's house *W*.
5. If a square represents one block, how many blocks must Patrick walk to get to Whitney's house without traveling diagonally? 12 blocks

Friday WEEK 7 91

Page 92

Geography

Landscape of Asia

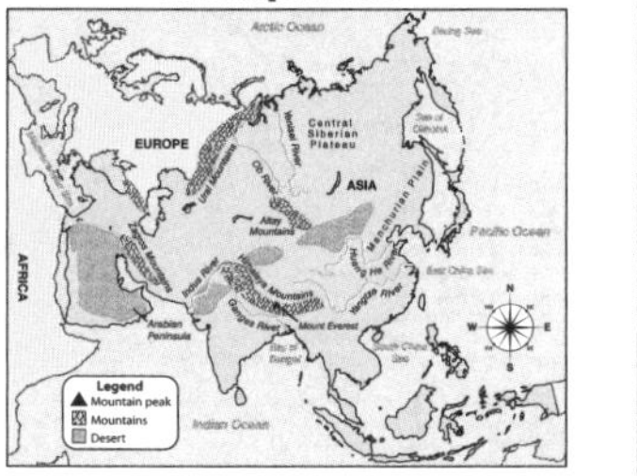

1. Which desert is between the Altay Mountains and the Manchurian Plain? **Gobi Desert**
2. Which mountain range is the main division between Asia and Europe? **Ural Mountains**
3. What is the name of the landform that is east of the Yenisei River? **Central Siberian Plateau**
4. In which direction are the Himalayas from the Zagros Mountains, southeast or southwest? **southeast**
5. Which river is directly north of the Yangtze River? **Huang He River**
6. Which landform covers the Arabian Peninsula? **Arabian Desert**

West of Greenwich — Longitude West of Greenwich

A 120° B 150° C 180° D 150° E 120° F 90°

92 Friday

Week 8

Page 95

Read It! Nonfiction

Read the article. Then answer the questions.

Flowers for Dinner

Flowers might look pretty on the dinner table. But what about serving them for dinner? In many cultures all around the world, people eat and enjoy a variety of flowers in their food.

The purple flowers of the lavender plant add a sweet lemon taste to chocolate cake or ice cream. Pansies, which have a grassy flavor, are a delicious addition to green salads. Bright yellow dandelion petals look cheerful when sprinkled over rice. Squash blossoms can be fried or stuffed with cheese. And the flowers of plants such as jasmine and chamomile are commonly used to make tea.

Does snacking on flowers sound weird? You may have eaten flowers already without realizing it. Several vegetables, such as cauliflower and broccoli, are actually flower buds. Artichokes, if left on their stalks, form fuzzy purple blooms. And asparagus tips open into small, pale green or white flowers.

If you're interested in eating flowers, be sure to learn about the plants first. Not every flower is safe to eat. The best way to find a tasty—and safe—flower is to visit your local grocery store.

1. **How are broccoli and lavender similar?**
   - Ⓐ Both have a lemon taste.
   - ● Both are flowering plants.
   - Ⓒ Both are used for tea.
   - Ⓓ Both have purple flowers.
2. **Why should you learn about a plant before eating its flower?**
   - ● to make sure the flower is safe to eat
   - Ⓑ to find out how to serve the flower
   - Ⓒ to learn more about other cultures
   - Ⓓ to find out how the flower tastes
3. **What is the main idea of the third paragraph?**
   - Ⓐ Eating flowers is weird.
   - Ⓑ Plants produce flowers of different colors.
   - ● Some vegetables are flower buds.
   - Ⓓ The flowers of some plants are used for teas.
4. **What is the main idea of the passage?**
   - ● Many flowers can be eaten.
   - Ⓑ Flowers are often eaten with desserts.
   - Ⓒ Many people eat flowers without realizing it.
   - Ⓓ Flowers are tastier than vegetables.

Monday WEEK 8 95

Page 96

Write It Right

Rewrite each sentence and correct the errors.

1. we read the declaration of independence in hour class
   We read the Declaration of Independence in our class.
2. nashville tennessee is the capitol of that state
   Nashville, Tennessee, is the capital of that state.
3. a trip to the museum of natural history is a reel treet
   A trip to the Museum of Natural History is a real treat.
4. josh asked can you come with me to the libary tomorrow
   Josh asked, "Can you come with me to the library tomorrow?"

MATH TIME

Complete the order of operations problems. Do the problem inside the parentheses first. Next, do multiplication and division from left to right. Then do addition and subtraction from left to right.

1. 9 x (5 + 3) = 72
2. 6 ÷ (6 − 3) = 2
3. 15 − (10 ÷ 2) = 10
4. 25 ÷ (10 − 5) = 5
5. 4 x 5 − (6 ÷ 2) = 17
6. 4 x (5 + 6) ÷ 2 = 22
7. 17 − 2 x (5 − 3) = 13
8. 16 x (4 x 2) = 128
9. 18 ÷ 9 + (6 ÷ 3) = 4
10. 3 + (6 + 3 − 5) ÷ 2 = 5
11. 45 − (5 x 5 + 10) = 10
12. 16 + (90 ÷ 5) = 34

96 Monday

Page 97

SPELL IT

Silent consonants are letters in a word that are not pronounced when the word is spoken.

Circle the silent letters in the spelling words for the week. Then write each word and draw a line between its syllables. Use a dictionary to help you if necessary. The first one has been done for you.

1. plumber — plumb|er
2. signpost — sign|post
3. chalkboard — chalk|board
4. shipwreck — ship|wreck
5. condemn — con|demn
6. castle — cas|tle
7. exhaustion — ex|haus|tion
8. pneumonia — pneu|mo|nia
9. doubtful — doubt|ful
10. doorknob — door|knob
11. wholesome — whole|some
12. honorable — hon|or|a|ble

In My Own Words

Invent an unusual new sandwich to be served at the school cafeteria. Name all the ingredients and explain how to prepare the sandwich.

Sample answer:
My unusual sandwich would be Chinese beef and broccoli on a toasted sesame seed bun. Start by toasting the bun. Then put beef and broccoli that has been marinated in teriyaki sauce on the bun. Add shredded cabbage and cooked sweet onions to complete the sandwich.

Tuesday WEEK 8 97

Page 98

LANGUAGE LINES

A prefix is a word part that comes before a base word and changes the meaning of the word. The prefixes in-, im-, il-, and de- mean "not" or "opposite of."

Complete each word with the correct prefix. Use a dictionary if necessary.

1. A person who is not active is **in**active.
2. If you remove the value from something, you **de**value it.
3. An act that is not legal is **il**legal.
4. A person who is not mature is **im**mature.
5. Something that is the opposite of activated is **de**activated.
6. A person who is not patient is **im**patient.

MATH TIME

A. Find the area of the circles. The first one has been done for you.

$A = \pi \times r^2$ (area = 3.14 x radius²)

1. r = 3: $A = \pi \times r^2$; $A = 3.14 \times (3 \times 3)$; A = 28.26
2. r = 4: A = 50.24
3. r = 6: A = 113.04

B. Find the circumference. The first one has been done for you.

$C = \pi \times d$ (circumference = 3.14 x diameter) or $C = 2 \times \pi \times r$ (circumference = 2 x 3.14 x radius)

1. d = 16: $C = \pi \times d$; $C = 3.14 \times 16$; C = 50.24
2. r = 4: C = 25.12
3. r = 12: C = 75.36
4. d = 20: C = 62.8

98 Tuesday

Page 99

Read It! Fiction

Read the story. Then answer the questions.

Disturbing the Peace

It was a beautiful spring morning on Lake Powell. Birds chirped and the trees rustled in the chilly morning breeze. Gentle waves moved across the surface of the clear blue water. Emma sat on the dock with her history book in her lap, occasionally looking out at the peaceful lake.

Suddenly, running footsteps came from behind, and a voice shouted, "Kowabunga!"

Before Emma could move an inch, her best friend Martha jumped directly over her head. Martha was shrieking with laughter as she jumped into the water. The cold water splashed all over Emma and soaked her.

As Martha swam back to the dock, Emma was wiping her face. "You said you'd never do that again!" Emma declared.

Martha pushed the hair out of her eyes and shrugged. "I said I wouldn't splash you at the pool, Em. We're at a lake now. And, come on, how much studying do you need to do on this trip? You've been reading all morning." Martha splashed the water playfully. "Come on, jump in! The water's great."

Emma sighed and closed her book. She would have to learn about pioneers along the Oregon Trail another day. The cool spring air was giving way to the summer sun. And besides, her best friend was just begging to be beaten in a race across the lake.

1. **What is the author's main purpose in writing the story?**
   - Ⓐ to persuade people to read history books
   - ● to tell a realistic story about friends
   - Ⓒ to demonstrate how to swim in a lake
   - Ⓓ to inform people about Lake Powell
2. **Why does the author describe the setting in the first paragraph?**
   - ● to create a peaceful mood
   - Ⓑ to show the main character's problem
   - Ⓒ to establish a mystery
   - Ⓓ to encourage readers to like Emma
3. **What does the author want you to think about Martha?**
   - Ⓐ that she is careful and considerate
   - Ⓑ that she is nicer than Emma
   - ● that she is more playful than Emma
   - Ⓓ that she is angry and bored
4. **The purpose of the last paragraph is to show that Emma ______.**
   - ● will join Martha in the lake
   - Ⓑ will continue reading her book
   - Ⓒ is annoyed with Martha's splashing
   - Ⓓ does not like to swim

Wednesday WEEK 8 99

Page 100

Vo·cab·u·lar·y

A **suffix** is an ending added to a word or root that affects the word's meaning.

–ous, –ious: full of or possessing qualities of → **nervous**: full of nerves or anxiety
–al, –ial: relating to → **royal**: relating to kings and queens
–ic, ical: relating to → **electric**: relating to electricity

A. Write the letter of the word that matches each definition. You will use the letters in Activity B.

Answer	Definition		
O	1. full of nutrients	C. nutritous O. nutritious	B. nutrical F. nutrial
S	2. relating to nature	S. natural G. naturial	N. naturous A. naturical
U	3. relating to history	I. historal R. historial	K. histrious U. historical
O	4. full of wonder	W. wonderious P. wondrical	M. wonderal O. wondrous
Y	5. relating to buying and selling	T. commercic L. commercical	Y. commercial D. commercious
J	6. relating to comedy	J. comic V. comedious	C. comedial H. comedous

B. Unscramble the letters you wrote in Activity A to spell a word that means "full of happiness." Circle the word's suffix.

joy(ous)

C. Write a sentence using the word you spelled in Activity B.

Marcia's wedding was a joyous occasion.

100 Wednesday

Page 101

LANGUAGE LINES

A complex sentence contains one independent clause and one or more dependent clauses. Both clauses have a subject and a predicate, but dependent clauses do not express a complete thought.

In each complex sentence, draw one line under the dependent clause and two lines under the independent clause.

1. When a big snowstorm is predicted, we make a special trip to the grocery store.
2. The store is crowded because everyone has heard the weather forecast.
3. As my mom and dad shop for important supplies, I look for marshmallows.
4. Marshmallows and hot chocolate make a nice treat when you are snowed in.
5. If the electricity goes off, we will need flashlights and candles.
6. Unless the weather forecast is wrong, we will not have school the next day.
7. I like to help build a fire in the fireplace when there is a big storm.
8. We toast marshmallows in the fire until we go to bed.

In My Own Words

Describe an exciting experience you've recently had. Where were you? Who were you with? Include specific details about what happened.

Sample answer:
Recently, I was stuck in traffic with my mom. We were getting grumpy and wondering what the problem was, when we noticed a baby raccoon in the road! Cars were slowing down to make sure they didn't hit the raccoon. All of a sudden, the mother raccoon waddled into the road and nudged her baby to the other side. Then they both ran off.

Thursday WEEK 8 101

Page 102

Mind Jigglers

Spoonerisms

A. A *spoonerism* is a short phrase in which the initial sounds of the words have been switched, often with a humorous result. Find each spoonerism in the story and write the phrase correctly. The first one has been done for you.

One day, Timmy and his ~~sittle lister~~ little sister went to the playground. Timmy climbed up a ~~lig badder~~ big ladder to go down the ~~sleep stide~~ steep slide. Then he and his sister ~~hug a dole~~ dug a hole in the sandbox. After that, Timmy climbed to the top of the ~~bonkey mars~~ monkey bars and slid down the ~~pall tole~~ tall pole. On the ~~hay wome~~ way home, Timmy and his sister ~~bopped sty the puck dond~~ stopped by the duck pond. They saw a ~~dommy muck~~ mommy duck with her ~~dellow yucklings~~ yellow ducklings.

B. Think of a spoonerism for each phrase. Then use it in a sentence. Sample answers:

- water bottle: I took my bater wottle to the gym.
- grilled cheese: My favorite sandwich is chilled greese.
- math book: I need my bath mook for the algebra exam.
- bubble gum: Larissa chomped loudly on her gubble bum.
- bake cookies: Tom and his mom decided to cake bookies.
- take a shower: Every morning, I shake a tower to get ready.

Challenge: Write a sentence containing two spoonerisms that are not already on this page.

The Red Sox dealt the Cardinals a blushing crow when they won the Sorld Weries.

102 Thursday

Page 103

MATH TIME

Box and Whisker Plot

Olivia collected the following data about her classmates and their scores on the last spelling test:

64 86 78 85 100 85 76 94 88 85

She put the data into a graph called a Box and Whisker Plot. The graph looked like this:

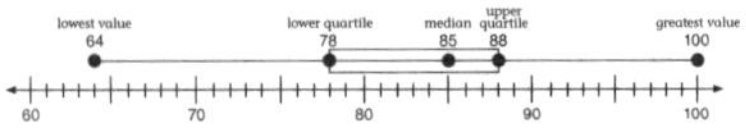

lowest value
64
lower quartile
78
median
85
upper quartile
88
greatest value
100
60
70
80
90
100

Now it's your turn. Follow the directions below to construct a Box and Whisker Plot for the data in the box, which shows the scores that Olivia's classmates received on their last math test.

80 72 100 80 70 84 88 90 98 78

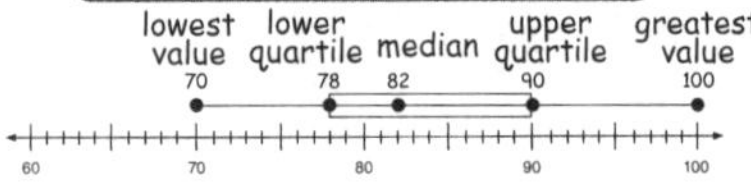

lowest value
70
lower quartile
78
median
82
upper quartile
90
greatest value
100
60
70
80
90
100

1. Write the scores on this line, from least to greatest value on the graph.
   70, 72, 78, 80, 80, 84, 88, 90, 98, 100
2. Draw dots to show the lowest value and the greatest value above the graph. Draw a line connecting the dots.
3. Draw a dot and label the median score. (When there is an even amount of numbers in a data set, take the average of the two numbers in the middle to find the median.)
4. Draw a dot and label the median of the lower range of the scores.
5. Draw a dot and label the median of the upper range of the scores.
6. Draw a box around the three median values.

Page 104

Geography

Countries of North America

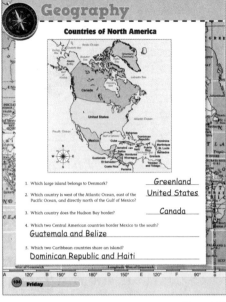

1. Which large island belongs to Denmark? Greenland
2. Which country is west of the Atlantic Ocean, east of the Pacific Ocean, and directly north of the Gulf of Mexico? United States
3. Which country does the Hudson Bay border? Canada
4. Which two Central American countries border Mexico to the south?
   Guatemala and Belize
5. Which two Caribbean countries share an island?
   Dominican Republic and Haiti

Week 9 Page 107

Read It! Nonfiction

Read the article. Then answer the questions.

A Sheltered Life

If you visit the animal shelter in Salinas, California, you'll see giant wooden cutouts of a dog and a cat. These signs were placed in front of the building to catch people's attention. The supersized cutouts make people curious and encourage them to visit the shelter—and maybe even adopt a pet. Each year, the Salinas shelter takes in about 2,000 dogs and 2,000 cats. The animals are either strays or are dropped off by people who couldn't take care of them. Of the 4,000 animals, some of them are eventually adopted into new homes. Some animals are transferred to other shelters. And, unfortunately, some cannot be saved because they are too sick or are considered dangerous.

Animal shelters provide food, medicine, and a safe place for animals to sleep. But they are not ideal homes. The shelters are loud, and the animals stay in small cages. The people who work at shelters do their best to care for the animals, but the animals do not always get the attention or exercise they need.

To prevent so many animals from becoming homeless, pet owners should take good care of their pets. One of the best ways to care for pets is to spay or neuter them. This surgery prevents cats and dogs from having more babies. And that reduces the number of homeless animals that end up in shelters.

1. **What is the passage mainly about?**
   - Ⓐ the city of Salinas, California
   - ● homeless animals in shelters
   - Ⓒ how to attract visitors to animal shelters
   - Ⓓ people who work at animal shelters
2. **Dogs in shelters probably do not get enough exercise because ______.**
   - Ⓐ the workers do not enjoy walking them
   - Ⓑ the workers think the dogs will be adopted soon
   - ● there are too many animals for the workers to care for
   - Ⓓ the workers are afraid of the dogs
3. **What is the result of spaying and neutering?**
   - Ⓐ More puppies and kittens are adopted.
   - Ⓑ Pets need less attention.
   - ● Fewer animals become homeless.
   - Ⓓ More people work at animal shelters.
4. **What can good homes offer that animal shelters cannot?**
   - ● plenty of personal attention
   - Ⓑ medical care
   - Ⓒ a safe place to sleep
   - Ⓓ food and water

Page 108

Write It Right

Rewrite each sentence and correct the errors.

1. mr smith the art teacher lended me the book about picasso
   Mr. Smith, the art teacher, lent me the book about Picasso.
2. noises especially loud ones are frightening at night whispered fred
   "Noises, especially loud ones, are frightening at night," whispered Fred.
3. my cat ollie naps wakes up and stretches and then she sleeps sum more
   My cat Ollie naps, wakes up and stretches, and then she sleeps some more.
4. kara hollered i hears you talking down there
   Kara hollered, "I hear you talking down there!"

MATH TIME

Julie lives on a farm with sheep and geese. There are 10 animals, and they have a total of 32 legs. How many of each animal are there on the farm? Complete the function table to find the answer. Then circle the row with the correct answer.

Sheep (S)	Geese (G)	Total Number of Legs Rule: (4 × S) + (2 × G)
9	1	38
8	2	36
7	3	34
6	4	32

Page 109

SPELL IT

Homophones are words that sound alike but have different spellings and meanings.

Circle the correct spelling word for each meaning.

1. toward the front — **forward** (circled) / foreword
2. an admiring remark — **compliment** (circled) / complement
3. at last — **finally** (circled) / finely
4. not moving — **stationary** (circled) / stationery
5. helpers — assistance / **assistants** (circled)
6. people under a doctor's care — **patients** (circled) / patience
7. a short introduction to a book — forward / **foreword** (circled)
8. paper used to write letters — stationary / **stationery** (circled)

In My Own Words

If you had to decide between living without a television or living without junk food, which would you choose? Explain your choice.

Sample answer:
I would much rather live without junk food than TV. There are many very tasty foods that are not considered junk and, in fact, are healthy choices. But there are so many programs on TV that I would miss very much if I could not watch them. Plus, I watch movies and play video games using the TV, too.

Page 110

LANGUAGE LINES

It is important to stay with the same verb tense from one sentence to the next. The tense should change only if the sentences are referring to different points in time.

Underline the verb in the first sentence. Fill in the blank in the second sentence with the correct tense of the word in parentheses.

1. Brad reports on school events. Mia takes (take) photographs for the paper.
2. The story about the cafeteria was interesting. It described (describe) all the menus.
3. Brad named the "crumble burger" the worst dish. He called (call) it "icky."
4. The paper will run a story on the library next month. I will write (write) it.
5. I am writing about fines for overdue books. Next year, the library will raise (raise) fines.

MATH TIME

A. Find **x** in each problem by adding or subtracting the same value on both sides of the equation.

$x - 6 = 3$ $x - 6 + 6 = 3 + 6$ $x = 9$	$x + 2 = 7$ $x + 2 - 2 = 7 - 2$ $x = 5$

1. $x + 4 = 5$ $x =$ 1
2. $x + 6 = 8$ $x =$ 2
3. $x - 5 = 12$ $x =$ 17
4. $x - 4 = 7$ $x =$ 11

B. Find **x** in each problem by multiplying or dividing the same value on both sides of the equation.

$y \div 6 = 3$ $y \div 6 \times 6 = 3 \times 6$ $y = 18$	$2y = 8$ $2y \div 2 = 8 \div 2$ $y = 4$

1. $6y = 24$ $y =$ 4
2. $3y = 18$ $y =$ 6
3. $y \div 1 = 7$ $y =$ 7
4. $y \div 8 = 6$ $y =$ 48

Page 111

Read It! Fiction

Read the story. Then answer the questions.

Mira's Visit

From the moment the airplane touched down at the Hong Kong airport, Mira knew she was in for an adventure. The busy airport was full of people bustling about. The people looked like they came from all over the world. Mira heard bits of conversation in many different languages.

Mira and her parents hurried to the hotel, where they checked in and dropped off their luggage. They were eager to begin exploring the city. Mira's dad brought a map and a detailed plan of what sights they would see.

The first stop on the list was the Hong Kong Wetland Park, just outside the city. The peaceful park had lots of places to walk, and Mira enjoyed sketching pictures of wildlife, including a crocodile lounging beside a private pool. On the train back to the city, the family marveled at the towering skyscrapers. Next, they stopped at the Science Museum, where Mira and her mom visited the World of Mirrors exhibit. After a lunch of local treats from a street-food cart, the family rushed to Victoria Harbor for the "Symphony of Lights." In the light show, beams of light were projected onto the buildings around the harbor and reflected off the calm waters below.

The family returned to the hotel, ready for a good night's sleep. Mira looked forward to another day of fun in Hong Kong. She was amazed to think of all they had done on their first day!

1. **What did Mira and her family do before exploring Hong Kong?**
   - Ⓐ They ate a meal at a street cart.
   - ● They left their luggage at the hotel.
   - Ⓒ They marveled at the city's skyscrapers.
   - Ⓓ They rode on a train.
2. **What did the family plan to do first?**
   - Ⓐ see a light show at the harbor
   - Ⓑ go to a science museum
   - ● go to a wildlife park
   - Ⓓ enjoy lunch
3. **When did the family eat lunch?**
   - ● after leaving the Science Museum
   - Ⓑ before visiting the World of Mirrors exhibit
   - Ⓒ after watching the "Symphony of Lights"
   - Ⓓ after taking a nap at the hotel
4. **When did Mira first realize that Hong Kong was probably a busy city?**
   - Ⓐ when she sketched a crocodile
   - Ⓑ when she saw the towering skyscrapers
   - Ⓒ when she and her family returned to the hotel
   - ● when she and her family arrived at the airport

Page 112

Vo·cab·u·lar·y

Roots are word parts that form the base of words and can give clues to a word's meaning.

viv = life nov = new clin = lean gen = birth

A. Underline the root in each word in the box. Then write the word that matches each clue. Use a dictionary if necessary. The number under each word will be used in Activity B.

gene vivid novice survive innovation novel inclined recliner genealogy

1. someone who is a beginner: novice (5)
2. a record of your ancestors: genealogy (7)
3. a biological unit of heredity: gene (3)
4. new, different, or unusual: novel (3)
5. leaning in one direction: inclined (1)
6. brightly colored: vivid (3)
7. to continue to live: survive (5)
8. creative and new: innovation (6)
9. a furniture piece that can be adjusted to lay back: recliner (4)

B. Look at the number below each word in Activity A. Count that number of letters from the beginning of the word and circle the letter. Read the circled letters from top to bottom to reveal a word that means "sociable." Write the word below and circle its root.

convivial

Page 113

LANGUAGE LINES

The antecedent of a pronoun is the noun or nouns that the pronoun refers to or replaces.

The antecedent is underlined in each sentence or pair of sentences below. Write the correct pronoun on the line to match the antecedent.

1. Students are excited about the class business. They are making greeting cards.
2. Amanda got the idea for the cards. She has a card-making program at home.
3. The business should be simple to run. Here is how it will work.
4. Amanda will make some sample cards, and they will be shown to customers.
5. Omar will be in charge of taking orders for cards. He will collect all the orders.
6. Students working with Trisha will then make the cards. She is a good artist.
7. The cards will be delivered to the customers, at which time money will be collected from them.
8. I would like to be a part of this class enterprise. It sounds exciting to me.

In My Own Words

Who or what makes you laugh? Why?

Sample answer:
My best friend Sabrina makes me laugh. She is always telling jokes, talking in silly voices, or just being a big goofball. I can't help but smile whenever she is around.

Page 114

Mind Jigglers

Abbreviations and Acronyms

Below are some common and uncommon abbreviations and acronyms used in text messaging. Use the numbers below to match each abbreviation at the bottom of the page with its meaning.

1. See you later!
2. high-five
3. Bye for now!
4. Excuse me.
5. are you
6. tomorrow
7. Oh, I see.
8. by the way
9. rolling on the floor laughing
10. I don't know.
11. anyone
12. nice to know
13. better known as
14. be back in a bit
15. two cents
16. no big deal
17. tons of time
18. Did you see that?
19. thinking of you
20. wonder
21. on the other hand
22. for crying out loud
23. in my humble opinion
24. away from keyboard
25. too good to be true
26. Don't hold your breath.
27. You've got to be kidding.
28. What did you say?

15 O2   **8** BTW   **11** NE1   **19** TOY
6 2MORO   **1** CUL8ER   **12** NTK   **14** BBIAB
20 IDR   **18** DUST   **7** OIC   **4** XME
25 2G2BT   **26** DHYB   **21** OTOH   **28** WDYS
22 4COL   **9** ROFL   **13** BKA   **23** IMHO
2 ^S   **10** IDK   **5** RU   **24** AFK
3 BFN   **16** NBD   **17** TOT   **27** YG2BK

114 Thursday

Page 115

MATH TIME

Connect the Dots

Plot the ordered pairs of numbers in the order in which they are listed in each set below, and connect them with straight lines. Start each new set of points with a new line. The lines will reveal a picture. The first line has been drawn for you in orange.

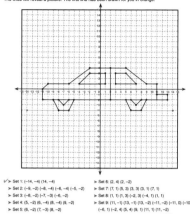

✓ Set 1: (−14, −4) (14, −4)
➤ Set 2: (−9, −2) (−8, −4) (−6, −4) (−5, −2)
➤ Set 3: (−8, −2) (−7, −3) (−6, −2)
➤ Set 4: (5, −2) (6, −4) (8, −4) (9, −2)
➤ Set 5: (6, −2) (7, −3) (8, −2)

➤ Set 6: (2, 4) (2, −2)
➤ Set 7: (7, 1) (5, 3) (3, 3) (1, 1)
➤ Set 8: (1, 1) (3, 1) (−2, 3) (−4, 1) (1, 1)
➤ Set 9: (11, −1) (13, −1) (13, −2) (−11, −2) (−11, 0) (−10, 1)
(−6, 1) (−2, 4) (5, 4) (9, 1) (11, 1) (11, −2)

Friday WEEK 9 115

Page 116

Geography

Europe's Bodies of Water

1. Which river flows into the Bay of Biscay? — **Loire River**
2. Which river is located on an island? — **Thames River**
3. Into which sea does the Volga River flow? — **Caspian Sea**
4. Which body of water connects the Black Sea to the Aegean Sea? — **Bosporus Strait**
5. Which river is farthest west in Europe? — **Tagus River**
6. Which five seas are part of the Mediterranean Sea? List them. — **Balearic Sea, Tyrrhenian Sea, Adriatic Sea, Ionian Sea, Aegean Sea**

116 Friday

Page 119

Read It! Fiction

Read the story. Then answer the questions.

The Amazing Phil

Sasha had simply wanted to get out of the car and stretch her legs. When she and her mom drove up to the ancient-looking gas station, neither of them was prepared to come face to face with a dinosaur. The sculpture loomed 20 feet over the car. It was a *T. rex*, and the green paint was peeling from its front legs, which dangled in the air. "I wonder who created this," she said, shading her eyes from the bright sun.

"I did," said a shaky voice nearby. Sasha turned around to see an elderly man propped up on a cane. He steadied himself and pointed one finger up toward the *T. rex* sculpture. "He's the Amazing Phil," the man said. "I built him in 1955, right after I opened the gas station. He brought in a crowd for a long time, back when people didn't drive so fast."

"It's a great sculpture," Sasha's mom half-lied. "I like the colors. So, what's your name?"

"My name's Phil, too," said the man. He leaned back on his cane. "My wife is inside. She just made a pecan pie. Do you ladies like pie?"

Sasha looked at her mom. Her mom looked up at the dinosaur and then gazed up the road for a few awkward seconds. Then she smiled and looked at Phil. "Pecan pie is our favorite," she replied, closing the car door behind her.

1. What is the author's main purpose for this story?
   Ⓐ to suggest a fun place to go
   ● to encourage readers to be nice to older people
   Ⓒ to make fun of older people
   Ⓓ to tell a scary story about dinosaurs

2. Which prediction could you correctly make based on the third paragraph?
   ● Sasha and her mom will be kind to the man.
   Ⓑ Sasha's mom will buy the sculpture.
   Ⓒ The dinosaur will come to life.
   Ⓓ The car will accidentally hit the dinosaur.

3. Why does the author include the detail that the dinosaur's paint is peeling?
   Ⓐ to scare the reader
   Ⓑ to show that the dinosaur is old
   Ⓒ to suggest that the dinosaur is ugly
   ● to imply that the dinosaur was poorly made

4. What will most likely happen next in the story?
   Ⓐ Sasha will stretch her legs.
   Ⓑ Sasha and her mom will drive away.
   ● Sasha and her mom will eat pie.
   Ⓓ Sasha will wait in the car.

Monday WEEK 10 119

Page 120

Write It Right

Rewrite each sentence and correct the errors.

1. the phone ringed just as mom was leafing the house
   The phone rang just as Mom was leaving the house.

2. my little couzen always says whats up
   My little cousin always says, "What's up!"

3. i just finished reding a book called through my eyes by ruby bridges
   I just finished reading a book called *Through My Eyes* by Ruby Bridges.

4. my littel sister wont stop bothering me to comes play out side
   My little sister won't stop bothering me to come play outside.

MATH TIME

Factor trees can be used to find the prime factorization of any number. The following is an example of a factor tree for the prime factorization of the number 18:

```
      18
     /  \
    2    9
        / \
       3   3
```
2 × 3 × 3 = 18

Draw a factor tree to find the prime factorization of each of the following numbers:

Sample answer: 16
8 × 2
4 × 2 × 2
2 × 2 × 2 × 2

Sample answer: 20
10 × 2
5 × 2 × 2

Sample answer: 24
8 × 3
4 × 2 × 3
2 × 2 × 2 × 3

120 Monday

Page 121

SPELL IT

Breaking a long word into **syllables** can help you remember the spelling.

Fill in the missing syllables to answer the clues with the spelling words for the week. If necessary, use a dictionary.

1. someone who makes maps: car**tog**ra**pher**
2. a square: rhom**bus**
3. an icy continent: Ant**arc**ti**ca**
4. the study of ancient relics: ar**chae**olo**gy**
5. completely surrounded by water: pe**nin**su**la**
6. the outside of a circle: cir**cum**fer**ence**
7. two or more countries: in**ter**na**tion**al
8. the natural world: en**vi**ron**ment**
9. half of Earth: hem**i**sphere
10. a rectangle: par**al**lel**o**gram
11. at a right angle: per**pen**dic**u**lar
12. love of country: pa**tri**ot**ism**

In My Own Words

What is your favorite subject in school? Why do you like it?

Sample answer:
My favorite subject is English because I love to read novels. I also enjoy writing essays and doing book reports.

Tuesday WEEK 10 121

Page 122

LANGUAGE LINES

Many words in English come from other languages, such as Arabic, Spanish, and Hindi.

Use your understanding of word meanings to match each word with its language of origin. Write the letter of the origin next to the English word.

g 1. absurd — a. from the Hungarian *gulyás*
a 2. goulash — b. from a Hawaiian word for a type of instrument
f 3. knapsack — c. from a Persian word meaning "market"
b 4. ukulele — d. from the French *liberté* meaning "freedom"
e 5. moccasin — e. from an Algonquin word for shoe
c 6. bazaar — f. from the Dutch word *knapzak*
h 7. cookie — g. from the French word *absurde*
d 8. liberty — h. from the Dutch word *koekje* meaning "little cake"

MATH TIME

Look at each set of fractions below and find the LCD (lowest common denominator).

1. 1/5, 2/3   LCD = **15**
2. 4/5, 6/7   LCD = **35**
3. 1/6, 2/3   LCD = **6**
4. 3/4, 9/10   LCD = **20**
5. 13/15, 1/20   LCD = **60**
6. 19/20, 1/24   LCD = **120**
7. 4/9, 8/5   LCD = **45**
8. 7/9, 5/11   LCD = **99**

122 Tuesday

Page 123

Read It! Nonfiction

Read the article. Then answer the questions.

Underground Mysteries

You may think that our knowledge of Earth is as solid as the ground beneath our feet. However, although scientists know some important facts about Earth's crust, many details are a mystery. To solve some of those mysteries, a group of Russian scientists drilled the deepest hole on the planet. Starting in the 1960s, researchers and special drillers began digging and drilling a hole. In the northwestern part of Russia, on the Kola Peninsula. Before they were done, the Kola Superdeep Borehole was more than 7.5 miles deep.

Researchers unearthed many fascinating facts by drilling this hole. Miles below the surface, they found rock that was full of water, like a sponge. Scientists believed that the water had formed from extreme pressure inside the rock. The researchers also found a layer of tiny fossils about four miles down, deeper than anyone expected to find fossils. Another surprise was that Earth was much hotter—over 350°F—as drillers dug deeper.

Eventually, the drilling area became so hot that the drill bits melted. New holes would close as soon as they were dug. Realizing that better technology was needed, the team stopped drilling in 1994. The deepest hole ever drilled by humans was abandoned, but researchers at new sites have continued to investigate the mysteries within Earth's crust.

1. Why were scientists able to learn new things from the Kola Superdeep Borehole?
   Ⓐ They had not tried drilling holes before.
   Ⓑ They devoted more money to the project.
   ● It was the deepest hole ever explored.
   Ⓓ Holes dug elsewhere did not reveal much.

2. Why did the project most likely need the skills of special drillers?
   Ⓐ The drilling project was unusual.
   Ⓑ The tiny fossils needed careful handling.
   Ⓒ Scientists knew about Earth's crust.
   ● Special drillers stopped the holes from closing.

3. What made the team realize they needed better technology to continue the work?
   Ⓐ The tools damaged the fossils.
   ● The heat melted the drill bits.
   Ⓒ Workers were not interested in the project.
   Ⓓ Water deposits ruined the drill.

4. The last sentence of the passage hints that
   Ⓐ Kola Superdeep Borehole was a waste of time
   Ⓑ superheated rock is found only in Russia
   Ⓒ other research sites were also abandoned
   ● discoveries are being made at other sites

Wednesday WEEK 10 123

Page 124

Vo·cab·u·lar·y

An idiom is a phrase that means something different than what its individual words mean.

Idiom: Who let the cat out of the bag?
What it means: "Who told the secret?" or "Who ruined the surprise?"
What it does not mean: "Who allowed a captured cat to escape?"

A. Rewrite each sentence by replacing the underlined words with the correct idiom from the box.

| fork over | way off base | give me the lowdown |
| tightfisted | shooting the breeze | take the reins |

1. Mr. Snively is a person who doesn't like to spend money.
   Mr. Snively is tightfisted.

2. Go ahead and explain everything to me about the surprise party.
   Go ahead and give me the lowdown about the surprise party.

3. No, you're not even close to being right about my age.
   No, you're way off base about my age.

4. They were chatting when the alarm sounded.
   They were shooting the breeze when the alarm sounded.

5. We had to pay a lot of money just to get into the amusement park.
   We had to fork over a lot of money just to get into the amusement park.

6. George will assume control on this project.
   George will take the reins on this project.

B. Write what a character on a TV crime drama might say to another character, using an idiom from Activity A.

Sample answer: Give me the lowdown on our next case, Sergeant.

124 Wednesday

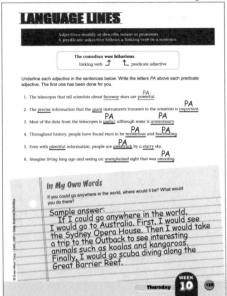

LANGUAGE LINES

Adjectives modify or describe nouns or pronouns.
A predicate adjective follows a linking verb in a sentence.

The comedian **was hilarious**.
linking verb ↗   ↖ predicate adjective

Underline each adjective in the sentences below. Write the letters *PA* above each predicate adjective. The first one has been done for you.

1. The telescopes that tell scientists about faraway stars are powerful. **PA**
2. The precise information that the giant instruments transmit to the scientists is important. **PA**
3. Most of the data from the telescopes is useful, although some is unnecessary. **PA** **PA**
4. Throughout history, people have found stars to be mysterious and fascinating. **PA** **PA**
5. Even with plentiful information, people are awestruck by a starry sky. **PA**
6. Imagine living long ago and seeing an unexplained sight that was amazing. **PA**

In My Own Words

If you could go anywhere in the world, where would it be? What would you do there?

Sample answer:
    If I could go anywhere in the world, I would go to Australia. First, I would see the Sydney Opera House. Then I would take a trip to the Outback to see interesting animals such as koalas and kangaroos. Finally, I would go scuba diving along the Great Barrier Reef.

Thursday   WEEK 10   125

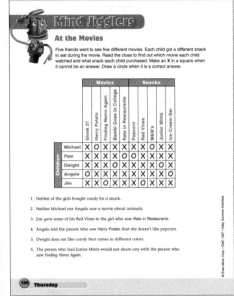

Mind Jigglers

At the Movies

Five friends went to see five different movies. Each child got a different snack to eat during the movie. Read the clues to find out which movie each child watched and what snack each child purchased. Make an X in a square when it cannot be an answer. Draw a circle when it is a correct answer.

	Shrek 27	Harry Potato	Finding Nemo Again	Bambi Goes to College	Rats in Restaurants	Popcorn	Red Vines	M&M's	Junior Mints	Ice-Cream Bar
Michael	X	O	X	X	X	X	O	X	X	X
Pam	X	X	X	X	O	O	X	X	X	X
Dwight	X	X	X	O	X	X	X	X	O	X
Angela	O	X	X	X	X	X	X	X	X	O
Jim	X	X	O	X	X	X	X	O	X	X

1. Neither of the girls bought candy for a snack.
2. Neither Michael nor Angela saw a movie about animals.
3. Jim gave some of his Red Vines to the girl who saw *Rats in Restaurants*.
4. Angela told the person who saw *Harry Potato* that she doesn't like popcorn.
5. Dwight does not like candy that comes in different colors.
6. The person who had Junior Mints would not share any with the person who saw *Finding Nemo Again*.

126   Thursday

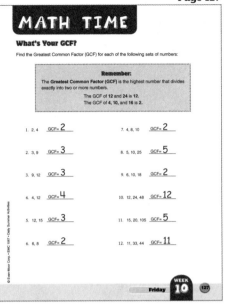

MATH TIME

What's Your GCF?

Find the Greatest Common Factor (GCF) for each of the following sets of numbers:

Remember:
The **Greatest Common Factor (GCF)** is the highest number that divides exactly into two or more numbers.
The GCF of **12** and **24** is **12**.
The GCF of **4, 10,** and **16** is **2.**

1. 2, 4   GCF= **2**   7. 4, 8, 10   GCF= **2**
2. 3, 9   GCF= **3**   8. 5, 10, 25   GCF= **5**
3. 9, 12   GCF= **3**   9. 6, 10, 18   GCF= **2**
4. 4, 12   GCF= **4**   10. 12, 24, 48   GCF= **12**
5. 12, 15   GCF= **3**   11. 15, 20, 105   GCF= **5**
6. 6, 8   GCF= **2**   12. 11, 33, 44   GCF= **11**

Friday   WEEK 10   127

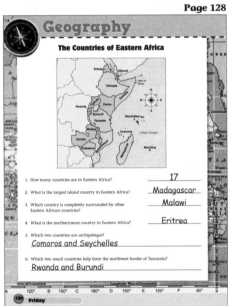

Geography

The Countries of Eastern Africa

1. How many countries are in Eastern Africa?   **17**
2. What is the largest island country in Eastern Africa?   **Madagascar**
3. Which country is completely surrounded by other Eastern African countries?   **Malawi**
4. What is the northernmost country in Eastern Africa?   **Eritrea**
5. Which two countries are archipelagos?   **Comoros and Seychelles**
6. Which two small countries help form the northwest border of Tanzania?   **Rwanda and Burundi**

128   Friday

summer journal